Advanced Praise For

I Don't Want to Die

"In a time when conversations around mental health are more important than ever, Tom Butero's book is both timely and essential. Tom brings clarity and compassion to one of the most difficult topics we face—suicide. With accessible language, real-world insight, and clinical relevance, this book guides readers through the complexities of assessment without ever losing its human touch. It's not just informative—it's a vital resource for anyone working to better understand and respond to suicide risk."
—Kathy Faucher, LICSW, BCN

"I Don't Want to Die is apropos for me and many of my colleagues who have patients in crisis. This book could be particularly useful for psychiatry and psychology students interested in the subject of depression and suicide."
—Anandhi Narasimhan, MD, Cedars Sinai Medical Center, Aviva Family and Children's Services, author of *How Concerned Should I Be? Questions Pertaining to the Developing Mind*

"This will be a meaningful and useful book for therapists and clinicians. Tom Butero's approach to this delicate subject is thoughtful, accessible, and much needed as more and more people are struggling with their mental health."
—Joan Childs, LCSW, family therapist, author of *Why Did She Jump?*

"Considering the turbulent world we live in, Tom Butero's new book will be a useful addition to existing literature on suicide. It should become a valuable primer for understanding how we can assess a person's susceptibility and take positive steps toward improving prevention tools."

—Mark Banschick, MD, family psychiatrist, author of *The Intelligent Divorce,* books one and two

"With its direct and personal approach, *I Don't Want to Die* engages professional and lay audiences who wish to address suicide prevention. Citing many helpful case examples, Butero draws from his years of clinical practice and research to formulate effective assessment and intervention strategies adaptable in any setting. These tools are essential for clinicians to utilize in their daily practice and can significantly increase one's comfort level and competency with suicide assessment. This can empower individuals and families, reduce stigma, and most importantly, save lives."

—Suzanne Patrone, LICSW, psychotherapist, East Side Counseling, Massachusetts

"It's refreshing to hear about a resource that imparts knowledge and inspires hope. This book goes beyond the traditional approach of simply providing information to engage readers on a deeper level. Its blend of education and inspiration will make it a valuable resource for medical students, residents, and clinicians alike."

—Lucyna Czarnota-Dolliver, MD, adult psychiatrist, Behavioral Health Department, Hawthorn Medical

"Having been touched both professionally and personally by suicide, I feel any tool which can be used to address the feelings of powerlessness which arise when dealing with a person who feels suicide is "the only solution" is extremely important.

"Both practitioners and families of vulnerable and depressed individuals can use the methods discussed in this book to "gain time" as one of the useful techniques to use in these difficult situations. The cyclical nature of suicidal ideation is emphasized. I had several patients who were unexpectedly prevented from completing their suicidal gesture, and they all were gratified to have lived and hopefully more motivated to remain in treatment."

—Ann M. Kenney LICSW, Retired after 30 years of clinical practice in inpatient and outpatient settings

"Tom Butero makes a significant (and readable) contribution to the understanding of suicide. For those who deal with suicide in a professional or personal setting, his organized, concise, and clear approach will enable us to be more effective in our interventions."

—John R. Jackson, MSW, retired Executive Director, Child & Family Services, Inc., New Bedford, MA

"In *I Don't Want to Die*, Mr. Butero's insights are critical in highlighting the link between alcohol and substance abuse and suicidal decision making and behavior in adolescents and young adults. His observations are especially relevant considering their developing brain, immaturity and potential for impulsivity. This book would serve as a useful guide to clinicians providing treatment as well as prevention services."

—David Patrone, LICSW, Certified Student Assistance Counselor (CSAC)

I Don't Want to Die:
A New Look at Suicide Assessment, Intervention, and Prevention
by Tom Butero, MSW

© Copyright 2025 Tom Butero

979-8-88824-748-8

All rights reserved. No part of this publication may be reproduced, stored in a retrieval system, or transmitted in any form or by any means—electronic, mechanical, photocopy, recording, or any other—except for brief quotations in printed reviews, without the prior written permission of the author.

Designed by Suzanne Bradshaw.

Published by

3705 Shore Drive
Virginia Beach, VA 23455
800-435-4811
www.koehlerbooks.com

I DON'T WANT TO DIE

A New Look at Suicide Assessment, Intervention, and Prevention

TOM BUTERO, MSW

VIRGINIA BEACH
CAPE CHARLES

To my dear wife, Marylou, whose support and belief in me has always inspired me.

And to the others who are too numerous to name: professors, mentors, colleagues, and family. Most importantly, to those who, I hope, I was able to help, even if in some small way, and who have taught me so much. Thank you.

CONTENTS

Introduction i
A Note from the Author iii
Prologue: "Crisis, Line Two" v

PART ONE:
DEPRESSION AND SUICIDE

   1. Types, Symptoms, and Influences 1
   2. The Emotional State 11
   3. Motivations For Suicide 16

PART TWO:
RISK FACTORS AND RED FLAGS

   4. Data and Demographics 25
   5. A Mental Status Exam 35
   6. Needle in a Haystack 37
   7. Specific Populations 47

PART THREE:
TOM'S SUICIDE ASSESSMENT TOOL

   8. Are You Feeling Suicidal? 59
   9. On the Flip Side 84

PART FOUR:
INTERVENTION

    10. The Question 89

    11. Three Levels of Intervention 94

    12. The Challenge of Providing
    Ongoing Treatment 120

    13. Emotional Landmines 123

    14. Contracting for Safety 136

    15. "The Question" Revisited 145

PART FIVE:
PREVENTION

    16. The Role of Traditional Media 149

    17. Social Media 151

    18. Suicide Prevention in Schools 154

    19. Some Closing Thoughts 162

About the Author 167

References 169

Introduction

A while back, I did a training on suicide assessment for a group of outpatient clinicians at a family service agency. Before I started, one of the clinicians asked me what model of suicide assessment I would be using.

I assumed she meant which of the more recent prepackaged, catchy, or "acronym" named assessment tools I would be presenting. I thought about the question for a minute and answered that I would be presenting "Tom's" suicide assessment model.

I cannot tell how or why I became interested in this topic. Often, people become interested or involved in a certain topic or issue because of firsthand experience, like the cancer survivor who becomes an advocate for research funding or the military veteran who becomes a counselor at a VA outreach center.

Have I ever attempted suicide? No. Have I contemplated taking my own life? I suppose at some point but not for a long period of time. We all have thoughts of suicide. Like me, those thoughts may be fleeting and never return, but it will happen. It's a normal part of living.

Suicide is one of the most preventable causes of death we know of—perhaps *the* most. Because of that, I believed it was my obligation to learn everything about the subject and put that knowledge to use in service to my clients. And my time has now come to pass on to others what I have learned.

But please understand that I cannot be all things to all people. There are certain topics I have not included, mostly out of a lack of adequate expertise. Seek guidance where you need.

Prior to writing this, I had a doctor's appointment. Nothing major, just my six-month checkup. He asked me what I have been up to, and I told him about this book. He said, "It's good you're doing this because you have a lot of knowledge that needs to be shared with others."

Who am I to argue with my doctor?

A Note from the Author

After poring over early drafts, my developmental editor came to me with a two-word, conceptual description of suicide: mysterious and elusive. I added a third: enigmatic.

People don't generally understand the dynamics, intricacies, and inner workings of the suicidal act. Uncovering its mystery requires one to understand that suicide is a behavior like any other. It is based on thoughts, feelings, and decisions. Like any behavior that may necessitate some type of intervention, a suicide attempt can be prevented.

As you will see, only in rare cases will a suicidal individual directly communicate their feelings to anyone. Unless someone has communicated their ideation or attempted suicide, most of us do not walk around wondering if someone we know is thinking about killing themselves.

Parents, for example, worry about their child's drug or alcohol use, sexual behavior, and their choice of friends. They worry about how they dress, how they wear their hair, makeup, tattoos, piercings. Most parents don't worry about whether their child is suicidal.

Being educated about the warning signs and risk factors can prevent suicide.

The enigmatic nature leaves us with unanswered questions, especially when a person completed their suicide. There are instruments, such as a psychological autopsy, that can help, but *why* someone chose to die by suicide can never be definitively answered.

Since the nature of suicidal ideation is so personal, we need to understand the uniqueness of each ideation. In doing so, we may understand the broader *why* of their decision.

Certain elements are repeated in sections or chapters of this book. While this may seem redundant, keep in mind that suicide's mysterious, elusive, and enigmatic nature demands that we revisit and reconsider different contexts to create clarity and emphasis. It's all part of trying to better understand and respond to the behaviors of those in need of our help.

Prologue:

"CRISIS, LINE TWO"

It was a nice spring day in Granite City, Illinois. I was part of the crisis team at the local mental health center. There were five of us on the team, including Ron, the program director, Susan, the clinical supervisor, and my teammates, Carla and Pat.

Brenda, who managed the front desk, ran it like it was the helm of the Starship Enterprise. She was unflappable when it came to incoming calls, clients checking in for appointments, and staff needing this or that.

At twenty-five, just a year out of college, I was on call for incoming crisis calls. I had barely finished my coffee when I heard Brenda's announcement over the intercom.

"Crisis. Line two."

Those three words put me on high alert. I picked up the receiver and pressed line two.

"This is Tom. How can I help you?"

"I took all of my pills."

Deep breath. Okay now. Jump in.

"Okay. Can you tell me your name?"

"Don."

I immediately knew who he was, having sat in on a couples' session with him, his wife, and their therapist the previous week.

"Okay, Don, do you know what you took?"

"Barbiturates. All of them. I took them all."

I was the youngest member of our team, but I had some experience. I'd been introduced to crisis intervention, suicide, and suicide prevention at George Williams College, a small liberal arts school in Downers Grove, Illinois. Williams founded the YMCA, and the school initially specialized in training students for careers in the Y movement. Later, it expanded, offering undergraduate and graduate degrees in human services, counseling, social work, and physical education. That is where it all began for me.

As a freshman, I volunteered at an on-campus drop-in center/hotline. We were trained in basic crisis intervention techniques. We were also taught how to intervene in specific situations, including suicidal crises, which intrigued me, but at the time, I needed to prioritize my coursework, so I put my newfound interest on the back burner.

Still, the question of *why* people choose to end their lives lingered. Maybe it was natural curiosity. Maybe it was a puzzle to solve. Whatever the reason, I wanted to understand the subject and find an answer. I revisited that question during my tenure at the mental health clinic.

Perhaps it was serendipity when, in 1975, I was accepted to VISTA (Volunteers in Service to America), a federal program often described as the domestic Peace Corps.

You volunteered for a year, living and working in some of the most poverty-stricken parts of the country, performing grassroots work, such as agricultural development, adult primary education, welfare rights, and improving access to basic services, like health care. You survived on a subsistence salary to cover rent, food, and general living expenses.

My placement at the clinic was a departure from VISTA's customary volunteer assignments. My coworker, Carla, was also from VISTA, and the rationale for placing us there was twofold. First, Madison County, Illinois, was one of the poorest in the state, ranking among the lowest 10 percent of per capita income. That was the major criteria used by Action, the parent organization that administered VISTA, Peace Corps, and related programs, to determine which communities were eligible for services.

My assignment was to replace another volunteer who had completed his service. The fact that the clinic continued to have us there brings me to the second reason for our presence.

A twenty-four-hour crisis team is essential to any mental health program. Unfortunately, that concept had not yet been recognized by those in power, and funding was slim. Having two VISTA volunteers on the team was economical for the clinic and the community to augment the salaried members of the team while demonstrating the ever-growing need for the service.

For me, it was one of the most positive and impactful experiences of my career.

The application asks you to define your interests and where you would like to be placed. I described my college experience and my interest in crisis intervention. Since I wanted to explore the country, I indicated my interest in being placed anywhere west of the Mississippi River.

Granite City was just a few miles from the east bank of the Mississippi. Close enough, I guess. Besides, the experience I gained was invaluable.

My college experience and training prepared me for that crisis call with Don.

As I listened, I could tell he was clearly under the influence, becoming increasingly incoherent. The on-call room had a sliding glass window that opened to the crisis office.

I kept Don on the phone while I waved to my coworkers. On my ever-present notepad, I quickly wrote Don's name, and in large letters, I scribbled three words: OD! CHART! TRACE!

I tore off the page and handed it through the opening to Pat, who read it and handed it to Carla. Whatever they had been doing suddenly became unimportant.

Even though this was rare, especially during a daytime shift, Pat and Carla knew exactly what to do. After Pat alerted Ron, she headed to the records room, where she pulled Don's chart. She handed me the chart and pointed to Don's prescribed medications.

There was nothing in the record to indicate that Don had been prescribed any medication with a sedating effect, at least not by one of our docs, but he clearly had access to something.

As I stayed on the phone, Ron hovered behind me, listening, reading my notes, and making suggestions on my notepad. Susan worked with Pat and Carla.

Through the window, I could hear Carla speaking with a telephone operator. "We have a client who reports having taken an overdose. I need to speak with your supervisor and start a trace immediately." Carla was trying to keep calm. Me too.

Caller ID and digital resources we have today could have helped enormously, but this was 1976. Tracing a call took at least forty-five minutes, and despite what was depicted in TV shows, a guy with headphones doing electronic magic in five minutes didn't happen in real life.

Pat called 911 to alert EMTs so they could be ready to go.

"No, I don't know exactly what town," she said. "Probably somewhere local. We'll just have to take that chance that it's Granite."

By now, the whole building was aware. Therapists, case managers, and even our medical director gathered outside the on-call room, ready to help.

Our crisis program secretary thought enough to bring me a glass of water. I had forgotten how dry one's mouth can get during an adrenaline rush.

Still on the phone, Ron wrote me a note: "Ask him where he is."

Of course! How could I miss that? I thought to myself.

It seemed so obvious after I read the note.

"Where are you, Don?"

"I don't know" was all he said.

"Do you know your address?" I asked, hoping for a response.

"We just moved here. I don't know the address," Don answered, much to my disappointment.

Computers were relatively new and took up a whole room. After an extensive search, which seemed like it took hours, even though it was only minutes, the phone company reported to Pat that they did not have any information under Don's name in their system.

Now it felt like everything was working against us. We learned later that the new phone number was not in his name.

In Don's groggy state, I heard him repeat something. "I don't want to die."

A breakthrough? I thought. "That's good, Don." *Is that the right thing to say?* "Listen, Don, we're going to do everything we can to make sure that doesn't happen. You can help me, though. Can you think of anything that might help us find you?"

"I'm trying . . ." was all he could say. Don's speech got more slurred. Then, he almost shouted, "Oh, God! I don't want to die!"

Don was starting to fade, and I started yelling his name into the phone, hoping he was still holding the receiver to his ear. "I'm here," he all but mumbled.

"Okay." *That's a relief.* "Listen, Don, can you stand?"

I thought that getting him to move around might keep him from passing out. Then again, in his unsteady condition, I was afraid he might fall. "Never mind, Don. Whatever you do, don't lie down. Try to stay sitting, okay?"

I could almost hear Don nodding. "Okay, I'll try," he said, a bit more coherent.

Amid the controlled chaos, Pat passed me a note: *Can he read the number on the phone?*

Back then, when a new phone was installed, the number was placed under a plastic cover on the face of the phone. I gave Pat a thumbs-up and asked Don. "I think so."

Clearly, Don was shaky and unsure. He tried reading the numbers but was struggling.

Ron suggested I have him repeat them a few times to be sure. Finally, Don read the same set of numbers three times in a row, and I felt as sure as I could that I had the right ones.

I passed the information to Carla, who was still talking with the telephone company. She read the number to the supervisor, who was able to get the name and address on the account. Carla passed it to Pat, who handed it to me through the window. Ron took the chart.

"Here it is," Ron said. "It's his wife's name. That's got to be where he is."

I shouted into the phone, hoping Don would confirm he was at home. At this point, he must have passed out, as I was no longer able to elicit a response.

"Don!"

I kept yelling his name, to no avail. The line was still open. After what seemed like forever, I heard another voice on the other end.

Carla!

"We're here."

That's all she said, and, for the first time, I sat back in my chair. Once we had Don's address, she and Pat had driven there, where they met the police and EMTs. The police broke into the apartment so the EMTs could tend to Don.

"He's unconscious," Carla said. "The EMTs told me that his eyes rolled back, which is not a good sign, but they think he's going to survive."

As I hung up the phone, I stood up, took a deep breath, and turned to Ron.

"They got him. They think he's going to be okay."

Ron shook my hand. "Good job." That was all he needed to say.

I stood up, stretched, and stepped out of the phone room. There were smiles all around and several pats on my back. This was a team effort, though, and I was just one cog in the wheel.

Don survived. I met him a week later when he and his wife came in for their therapy appointment. They were both very thankful.

All things considered, I would not have traded my VISTA experience for anything. I learned more about working with people in crisis in that year than four years of college and two years of graduate school.

Beyond the "hands-on" experience I garnered, the clinic had a great library, and I read everything related to suicide and suicide prevention that I could get my hands on, including Norman L. Farberow and Edwin S. Shneidman's *The Cry for Help*, Émile Durkheim's *Suicide*, and a whole collection of journals.

For me, these were the foundations I needed to better understand the dynamics behind suicidal behavior and its prevention.

My reading and research continued well beyond that year, and during my endeavors, I discovered the importance of understanding other concepts and conditions that directly relate to the issue of suicide.

The primary one is depression, so that is where we will begin. Before we do, I want to thank everyone at VISTA and the mental health center in Granite City, Illinois. And of course, Don, whose courageous struggle lies at the heart of this book.

PART ONE:

DEPRESSION AND SUICIDE

1. TYPES, SYMPTOMS, AND INFLUENCES

UNDERSTANDING DEPRESSION IS a vital part of understanding why someone commits suicide. While a common myth claims that people who commit suicide are "crazy," conventional diagnostic and statistical manuals define depression as a mental disorder, which can be categorized as a mood disorder, which is just what it sounds like—a mental disorder that affects one's mood.

Many mental health conditions include symptoms of depression, such as bipolar disorders (also classified as a mood disorder), post-traumatic stress disorder (PTSD), thought disorders, including schizophrenia, postpartum depression, acute trauma, and seasonal affective disorders, and anxiety (also considered a mood disorder, though a slightly different type in relation to its symptoms and possible origins).

Treatment approaches are typically specific to the type of disorder, but there are similarities, which specialists must determine as they offer treatment.

Depression and anxiety are two of the most common forms of mood disorders. Depression is characterized by several major symptoms that could go either way. For example, someone may suffer from a lack of sleep, or they may sleep excessively, anywhere from twelve to fourteen or more hours a day, and remain tired.

Appetite disturbance is also a symptom of depression, which can cause a lack of appetite or overeating. Many of us know someone who combats their depression by trying to eat away their feelings with a package of Oreos.

Other symptoms of depression include sadness, irritability, apathy, anhedonia, and a general loss of interest, caring, and motivation for almost anything.

Depression affects people in different ways. For example, adults tend to manifest most of what are considered "classic" signs of depression.

Adolescents, however, particularly adolescent boys, do not always exhibit these stereotypical signs. Almost by nature, adolescents experience emotional ups and downs. One minute, a teenager might appear happy, while the next minute, they might be anxious, agitated, sad, angry, depressed, or frightened. These so-called mood swings can be attributed to hormonal changes and the emotional upheaval of adolescence.

I remember a comic strip about a teenage boy named Kudzu. In one strip, Kudzu is walking along, looking normal. In the next panel, his eyes are bugged out, his hair is on fire, his arms and legs shoot out in all directions, and his mouth is wide open. In the next panel, he is walking along, looking like himself again. The caption read "Hormone Attack."

This is what makes diagnosing depression in adolescence difficult, along with many other potential psychiatric disorders. As mentioned, depression is particularly difficult to diagnose in adolescent boys. Depression in a fourteen- or fifteen-year-old boy is often exhibited by anger. We'll examine this more in chapter seven.

MANY FACES, MANY FORMS

Now, you can begin to see that depression has many faces and can be manifested in many different forms. Understanding the origins of depression for each person is just as important as understanding how that person is affected by their depression and how it manifests itself.

In general terms, depression comes in two forms. The first is classified as a depressive illness. This is a form of depression that has a specific psychophysiological foundation that can be traced to certain biochemical imbalances and shortages.

There is more and more evidence of genetic predispositions to depressive illness. We are also learning more about bipolar disorder and the potential risks that occur mostly during the depressive phase of the disorder.

The symptoms of a depressive illness usually include most, if not all, of those mentioned above. They can, however, be, and often are, of a much more severe nature. The best approach to treatment is a combination of medication and psychotherapy.

Talk therapy alone will not address the physiological aspects of the illness. Medications to treat depression have come a long way, especially in the last few years. Now we also have a family of supplemental meds that work in tandem with a primary antidepressant medication.

Medications to treat bipolar disorders, psychotic illnesses, and other biochemically induced depression have also seen significant advances in terms of their effectiveness.

In my experience, any type of depressive illness is less prevalent than a type of depression I refer to as being more reactive in nature. Don't misunderstand. A psychophysiological basis for a depression is serious and can carry an even higher level of risk for suicide than a reactive depression. This is mostly due to the severity of the depression. That said, the dynamics behind suicidal ideation or even an attempt are similar, despite the circumstances.

GRIEF AND DEPRESSION

In *On Death and Dying*, Elizabeth Kubler-Ross defines the five stages of grief. One of those stages is depression. I believe Kubler-Ross is referring to reactive depression; the person's depressive mood is a reaction to something that occurred in their life. I have found that this type can usually be traced to some form of loss.

Kubler-Ross talks about loss in relation to death. I suggest, however, that you expand your definition of loss and understand that the concept can be attributed to different experiences.

For example, relational breakups are a loss. Relocating can be a loss, cutting ties with close family, friends, and coworkers.

Loss can relate to how we function in certain areas of life. That straight A student, for example, who gets a C for the first time may experience a loss relative to their grade point average, class ranking, and sense of accomplishment.

The injured athlete who is forced to give up their sport experiences a loss. Developing a life-threatening illness can be seen as a loss of health and wellness.

These are examples of loss, but they are defined differently. I have seen that no matter what type of loss someone experiences, their reaction is akin to grief, as Kubler-Ross describes.

Thinking about loss in this way helped me identify varying degrees of grief. Defining a client's feelings in this context can help them comprehend the "normality" of their experience.

LOSS OF IDENTITY AND DEPRESSION

In the early 1980s, there was a sharp increase in unemployment in the US. You can draw your own conclusions as to the reasons behind it, but one factor stood out.

Many of the newly unemployed were professionals and upper-level managers in their fifties, who, after working twenty-plus years for the same company, were being laid off in large numbers. Many of them were men who also occupied traditional roles of husband and father and were often the primary source of income for their families.

At that time, I worked for an agency in an upper-middle-class suburban area of Chicago. While following local news and tracking other sources, we discovered that the communities we served seemed to have an inordinate number of men who fit the profile as I have described and found themselves newly unemployed.

In response to this phenomenon, I decided to organize a weekly support group for unemployed men. I wasn't trying to be discriminatory or exclusionary, but I was working with the theory that there were probably several issues, reactions, and concerns that these men would have in common with each other. This proved to be the case.

Our initial concerns about how a group like this would be received and whether we would get anyone to participate were put aside when fifteen men, ranging in age from their late twenties to early sixties, showed up to the first meeting.

Some returned after the first meeting, and others did not when they realized that the goal of the group was not to help them find a job but to help them deal with the emotional issues associated with their situation.

The group continued for more than a year, and as people came and went, we decided to include activities related to job seeking, such as role-playing interviews and videotaping them for review. At one point, we brought in an executive recruiter who explained what he looks for in a candidate and how to prepare a résumé and cover letter.

Over time, the group took on a life of its own. I knew it had become successful when they met without me while I went on vacation. Some members developed friendships that continued outside the group. A few even organized a group outing to a Cubs game.

The sense of loss (and depression) these men experienced was evident from the first day they walked into the group. The loss of their job was the most obvious trigger, but there was also a loss of income, security, and, in some cases, family. At least two members had their marriages end in divorce. Whether this was a result of their job loss is debatable, but it was likely a contributing factor.

We also saw an overriding loss of identity, which affected their sense of self-worth.

When new members joined the group, I asked everyone to introduce themselves.

"My name is Howard. I'm an engineer."

"I'm Frank. I'm a plant manager."

This is how it went. Each man identified himself through the lens of what they did for a living. They were architects, scientists, insurance executives, computer consultants, etc. Take those positions away, and they struggled to answer that question. Even though they were no longer doing that job, they would still define themselves in relation to their chosen profession.

The difficulty for many was how persistently they held onto that identity, which sometimes got in the way of their ability to seek employment in a different field. However, a few were able to apply hobbies or avocations to their job search.

There was no question that the group offered a much-needed outlet. As a clinician, I also observed them from a more detached perspective in relation to their emotions and behaviors.

It was amazing how some worked through their loss and grief, while others struggled.

Many of the most recently laid off men entered the group in a general state of denial and, later, anger. Many needed to vent about how unfair it was and how angry they were at their employer. At the same time, they talked about how this was a transitory situation and that they were sure they would have no problem finding a new job within a few weeks.

One new member was younger than most. James was married and had two young children. He came to his first meeting with a bit of bluster.

"This is just temporary," he said. "I'll be fine."

"Really?" said another member.

"I'm an accountant," James said. "They always need guys like me, so I'll be fine."

"Well, if that's the case, why are you here?" said Lawrence, one of the charter members.

James smiled. "My wife thought it might be a good idea. You know, maybe pick up a few tips. Gets me out of the house too. I think she wants me out of her hair."

This comment prompted a few smirks. *Do they appreciate his futile attempt at humor, or is this their way of warning, wait and see?* I thought.

After two weeks, then a month, and then six weeks, James was no closer to securing a job than his first meeting. He had a few interviews, but the candidate pool was too large.

Sensing his struggle, the other members tried to offer support.

"I'm beginning to think this is not going to be as easy as I thought," James said.

One of the members couldn't help but laugh. "You just now figuring that out?"

"Listen," Lawrence said. "I've been coming here for over four months. But I'm nowhere closer to finding a job than I was last summer."

James looked at him. "So, why do you keep coming? What's the point?"

"The point, my friend, is that it keeps us sane," said Lawrence. "Things are tough out there. You're just finding that out. But at least here, I can share my frustration and my anger with people who understand where it's coming from. Do you get angry?"

James looked puzzled. "Do I what?"

"Do you get angry? Do you blow up at people?"

Walt, another member piped in. "Are you sleeping? You look like you've lost a few pounds since I met you. Are you eating? I bet you aren't. Do you ruminate? Are you worried?"

"Okay, wait a second," James said. "What's with all these questions? What's any of this got to do with getting a job?"

Lawrence looked at me. "Tom?"

I looked at James and then at the rest of the group. "It's called grief," I said.

James shook his head.

"I don't get it."

I looked around the circle of chairs. "Gentlemen?"

One by one, they spoke up so quickly and pointedly that I almost couldn't keep up.

Lawrence, again, took the "podium." "James, when you first came here, you were in denial. We all saw it. You remember?"

He went on, "You were so sure you'd find a job right away. It never occurred to you that it might not happen that way. Now you're looking and sounding angrier."

"And maybe depressed?" another member offered.

The more they said, the more James looked sad, almost defeated. Lawrence had become the unofficial spokesperson for the group. He held up his hand as if to say *enough*.

"James, listen. We've all been there, exactly where you are. Tom has been our go-to guy to explain what it all means, but we've all been there."

"So, what are you saying?" James said.

"I'm saying that what you're going through is normal," said Lawrence.

Alex spoke up. "The good news is that you can get over it. I have. I came here in the same state as you are now, but I got past it."

"How?" James asked, now more interested.

Alex explained himself. "This group helped me. I was able to share what was going on inside. I got the support I needed from these guys to move on. You will too. You just have to let it go and realize that who you are doesn't have to be wrapped up in a job. Once you do that, the rest is easy."

James listened, but I wasn't sure he was getting it.

"Do you get what they're saying, James? Do you hear them?" I asked.

"I think so, but I'm not sure. But I don't understand how this helps me find a job."

Alex threw up his hands and sighed.

"Oh, you'll get it eventually. Just keep coming and listening and learning. You'll get it."

James finally did "get it." In fact, three weeks later, he found a new job. We weren't sure what happened, as he just stopped coming to the group. The following week, the local bakery delivered a box of goodies with a note from James, thanking us for everything.

This is how it went. New members would join the group, and I could almost pinpoint where they were in relation to their grief process. Almost invariably, reality would set in about how difficult it was to find a new job. That's when the depression phase often began to show.

Those who were able to work through that stage successfully and move on finally got to the final stage of acceptance. Interestingly, for many of them, it wasn't until they reached acceptance that they were able to find employment. I drew a very unscientific conclusion that being stuck in one of the earlier stages of grief was getting in the way of their ability to find new jobs.

Sometimes, I observed a member of the group as he got stuck in the depression phase of his grief process for what seemed like an inordinate length of time. At that point, I sometimes offered to meet with the person individually to discuss those feelings. When asked, they were forthcoming about whether they had experienced thoughts of suicide.

As far as I know, there were no attempts among any of the members, but a few of them were clearly having difficulty working through their depression. Some felt that they could benefit from one-on-one therapy. Boundaries being what they are, I would refer them to a colleague for ongoing individual work.

This group was a clear example of how a loss other than death can trigger a grief reaction. It also displayed how being stuck in the depressive phase can lead to suicide consideration.

ONE SIZE DOES NOT FIT ALL

Depression exists "in the eye of the beholder." Something perceived by one person as relatively inconsequential might be extremely troubling to another.

For example, consider an adolescent's experience of the loss of a pet. While most adults would react to this with sadness and loss, a young person may be more deeply affected.

Think about this. The dog is often a teen's most loyal friend. The dog doesn't care if they didn't clean their room. The dog doesn't care if they failed an exam. The dog is there every day to greet them with a wagging tail and kisses.

The loss of this lifetime companion can be traumatic for the adolescent.

Feelings are legitimate, no matter the situation. This is especially important for parents, spouses, etc., to understand and appreciate.

2. THE EMOTIONAL STATE

IT IS GENERALLY accepted that most people who attempt suicide are suffering from some form of depression. However, a subset of individuals with a thought disorder, usually in the form of psychosis, also attempt suicide. Some who have survived a suicide attempt often report having heard voices, typically known as command hallucinations, telling them to kill themselves.

Data from the National Institutes of Health and the World Health Organization speaks to the percentage of people with a thought disorder alone versus those with depression who make suicide attempts. Several studies found that persons suffering from a thought disorder also had a secondary diagnosis of depression. Most of the findings cited the role of depression as the mitigating factor for suicide. One article, in particular concluded the following:

> Affective dysfunction, including distress in response to hallucinations and delusions, was a key factor associated with suicidal ideation in individuals with psychotic relapse. Suicidal ideation in psychosis appears to be an understandable, mood-driven process, rather than being of irrational or "psychotic" origin.[1]

Another subset of at-risk populations is those who suffer from bipolar disorder. The highs and lows that accompany bipolar are risk

---

1—Fialko L, Freeman D, Bebbington PE, Kuipers E, Garety PA, Dunn G, Fowler D. Understanding suicidal ideation in psychosis: findings from the Psychological Prevention of Relapse in Psychosis (PRP) trial. Acta Psychiatr Scand. 2006 Sep;114(3):177-86. doi: 10.1111/j.1600-0447.2006.00849.x. PMID: 16889588.

factors for suicide. Here again, it is typically during the depressive phase of this syndrome when the person is most at risk.

That is not to say that suicide is not an issue for someone during a manic phase. The presence of risk factors and warning signs must be explored whatever the circumstance.

So, if we agree that depression plays a major role in relation to someone's suicidal feelings, what pushes them "over the edge" to the point of being actively suicidal?

HOPELESS, HELPLESS, AND WORTHLESS

In addition to feelings of depression and its associated symptoms, most people who are actively suicidal also find themselves in an emotional state characterized by three basic feelings.

» **HOPELESS**

This feeling relates to the person's belief that the problem or situation they find themselves in will never get better. They have a sense, albeit often misguided, that the feelings they are experiencing will never go away. You've no doubt heard the phrase "hopeless case."

I use the word "misguided" only because mental health providers know, based on experience and training, that no one is truly hopeless. The challenge for providers is to take care not to discount these feelings based on the belief that hopelessness is mostly a matter of perception rather than reality.

Keeping in mind that perception is 90 percent of reality, it is important to acknowledge the presence of hopelessness when it is reported by a client. The goal, then, is to help the client understand that these feelings can be addressed through a joint effort of therapy and, in some situations, medication. This is a difficult process with someone in the depths of depression.

There is a concept known as the installation of hope. As difficult as this may be with someone caught up in their own sense of doom, it *can* be an effective way of opening the door to ameliorating the feeling. The watchword here is "can." There are no guarantees that any sort of intervention will make things better.

» **HELPLESS**

For a person feeling suicidal, there is a strong sense of powerlessness and a total lack of control over anything, and anyone, associated with them. Actively suicidal individuals often report that they have tried everything to feel better or improve their situation and nothing has worked.

Depression also plays a big role in a person feeling stuck and unable to move emotionally—and even sometimes physically. Just like hopelessness, helplessness is often an obstacle to seeking treatment.

"How can you help me if I can't even help myself?" is often the question that someone brings to therapy.

I recall an old saying: "The harder I try, the behinder I get." Helplessness is self-defeating. It reinforces the sense of one's life being beyond their control. Possible reasons behind this include a lack of control due to external, uncontrollable factors and internal factors, such as a psychophysiological basis for one's depression that cannot be controlled without medication.

Helplessness becomes cyclical. The more helpless I feel, the more depressed I get. The more depressed I get, the more helpless I feel.

» **WORTHLESS**

Depressed people typically don't like themselves. Depression often triggers or exacerbates feelings of low self-esteem. We often see feelings of worthlessness manifested in a suicidal individual when they say that "everyone would be better off without me anyway."

Like hopelessness, feelings of worthlessness are often not based in reality. Remember George Bailey in *It's a Wonderful Life*? He says, "Yeah, if it hadn't been for me, everybody'd be a lot better off. My wife, and my kids and my friends."

George takes it a step further when he says he wished he had never been born, which is worthlessness taken to the next level. He soon learns that nothing could be further than the truth.

Dealing with issues related to worthlessness is difficult. You need to address the feeling in relation to someone's depression and suicidal ideation. Odds are you will probably have to dig deeper into what are most likely long-standing feelings of low self-esteem being intensified by depression.

Beyond these feelings, depressed and suicidal individuals often experience *tunnel vision*, a figurative phenomenon that refers to seeing things only in black-or-white.

There are no gray areas or alternatives. All they see is a dark tunnel with no light at the end. The approach here is to help the individual see that there are alternatives and gray areas that can be explored.

At one time or another, we all experience hopelessness, helplessness, and worthlessness. So, what pushes someone to the point of being suicidal while the rest of us cope with and overcome these feelings and get on with our lives?

The answer is simple but not easy. Some of us cope better than others with the inevitable impediments that life throws at us. Understanding and identifying coping skills, the importance of external support, and the constitutional factors that contribute to an individual's ability to overcome life's difficulties is a whole other book. Suffice to say that the better equipped we are to deal with stress and crises in our lives, the less apt we are to become depressed and/or suicidal.

A TOUGH ROAD

Anyone suffering from clinical depression faces a greater challenge in trying to cope with life's stresses. No matter how well prepared they believe they are, depression will inevitably make things more difficult.

Can a depression that is physiologically, biochemically, and/or genetically based be managed successfully? Absolutely! Through an individual's emotional strength, support from loved ones and friends, and targeted interventions, it can be accomplished, but it's a tough road to navigate.

Someone who suffers from a more reactive type of depression can also face what seems like an insurmountable mountain to climb. In either case, the seriousness of the depression must be evaluated as a vital component of any risk assessment.

In every seminar, presentation, and training program I do, I always make a prediction for everyone in attendance: At some point in our lives, all of us will entertain thoughts of suicide.

That does not mean you will ever attempt suicide. These thoughts may be fleeting and never return, but if it has not already happened, it will.

Suicidal thoughts and feelings are a normal part of everyone's existence. How one chooses to react to those feelings is one variable that determines one's level of risk.

So, why does suicide become a "solution" for some people? Think about whether someone can cope with depression and suicidal thoughts. Consider the intensity and overwhelming nature of those feelings and the precursor of depression and despair that some may feel in relation to any possible suicidal ideation.

3. MOTIVATIONS FOR SUICIDE

ASK FIFTY PEOPLE why they attempted suicide, and you will hear fifty reasons. However, most suicides and the motivation behind their attempts can be categorized in one of three ways.

The first and probably the main reason is to stop the pain. Sometimes, that pain is physical, such as an illness, injury, or disability. Most of the time, it is emotional.

Depression has often been described as emotional pain. You can often see it manifested physically in the way they carry themselves, in their facial expression, posture, or in their speech, and through symptoms like stomach disorders, headaches, etc.

THE STORY OF GREG

A forty-five-year-old man was referred to me after he had reportedly suffered a "breakdown" at his job as a case worker for the state welfare department. When I first met Greg, it was clear he was hurting. His shoulders were hunched over. He held his head down and walked with a slow, almost cautious gait. His speech was soft and measured. As he took the chair furthest from me, he pulled his legs up under the seat, crossed his arms, and stared at the floor.

"Greg, how are you doing?" Given his presentation, I retrospectively realized what an inane question that was. Still, I had to start somewhere.

He was finally able to look up at me, with difficulty. "I guess not so good. That's why I'm here, right?" he said softly.

"So it would appear," I offered. "I understand something happened at work. Can you tell me about it?"

"I kind of blew up. I remember just finishing a call. I put the phone down, and I guess I started throwing things from my desk up in the air. I didn't hurt anyone, did I?"

I shook my head. "Not from what I hear. Tell me, anything like that ever happen before?"

Greg looked up at the ceiling and paused. "No, nothing like that. I have been kind of depressed lately, though. You think maybe that had something to do with it?"

"Could be. How long have you been feeling this way?"

"A few weeks, maybe over a month. I can't say for sure. Geez, I just feel so desperate. I try to make myself feel better, but nothing works."

"How have you tried?" I asked.

Greg had tried exercising, going for walks, and treating himself by going out with his wife to a nice restaurant. Nothing seemed to help. "It seems like the more I try, the worse I feel. I get so frustrated. I just want these feelings to go away. My wife is worried about me. That only makes me feel worse, like I'm causing problems for her."

"Is this the worst it's been?" I asked.

Greg nodded. "Kind of. I mean, it's not any worse than before, but it's not any better either."

We talked about his symptoms, sleep habits, appetite, etc. Determining the root causes of his depression would come later. I was more concerned about Greg's immediate well-being. Finally, I had to say, "Greg. I must ask you something. I hope you'll be honest with me."

Before I could ask, he cut me off. "Have I thought about hurting myself? Is that what you want to know?"

"Yes. It's something I ask everyone. Just part of my overall assessment."

Greg admitted to having some thoughts of suicide, but he denied any active ideation. He had no plan, no means, and had not made any attempts. Still, he said the thoughts come and go. This was part of his depression and a cause for concern.

He agreed to continue to see me and follow up on a referral I made to a local psychiatrist for a medication evaluation. He assured me he was not suicidal, and I took him at his word.

Greg's case clearly shows how feelings of hopelessness and helplessness are related to the pain he experienced. Though he was not suicidal, nothing he did could make the pain go away. His frustration and desperation are what led to the incident at his job.

WHO IS IN CONTROL?

For some, suicide becomes a way of ending the pain. Permanently. It is not a strategy any of us would encourage, but there is no arguing the fact that it will make the pain go away.

Oftentimes, you will hear someone say, "I just want to stop hurting," "I want the pain to go away," or "I don't think I'll ever feel better." For many, it feels like their life is beyond their control. Of course, this begs the question, do any of us have control over our lives, or are we just along for the ride?

There have been times when I sat back and let life take me wherever it chose to go. And sometimes, I have felt totally in control of my life, and whatever I did and whatever happened was of my own choosing.

In certain circumstances, reality takes control of one's life, like terminal illness. In that situation, suicide may be seen as a way of taking control over what has become uncontrollable.

On the other hand, sometimes a lack of control or giving up control and using suicide to take it back is a power struggle more than anything else. I've seen this with adolescents.

Their attitude may go something like this: "You can tell me what to do, when to do it, and how to do it. You can tell me I have to stay in school, who I can and cannot hang out with, what time I have to be home, how to dress, or how much makeup I'm allowed to wear. You can try to restrict my online time (good luck). But you cannot make me go on living if I choose to die."

This sort of thinking usually goes on in the young person's head. Rarely would you see someone verbalize their feelings. When that happens, it's crucial to take some sort of action.

Such a scenario demonstrates an extreme perspective. The circumstances around the adolescent's suicidal feelings generally go beyond their parent's or anyone else's attempt to control them. At first glance, these power struggles might appear to be the major reasons for a young person's suicide attempt. There is more to it than that.

We need to go further and try to understand why these power struggles occur in the first place and why they seem to be so intense. Depression and low self-esteem are often present and are a contributing factor, but they may not always be obvious.

Emile Durkheim referred to one category of suicidal ideation as altruistic. This means that the motivation for one's suicide attempt is influenced either positively or negatively by another person or persons or some other outside circumstance.

The situation of a soldier throwing himself on top of an exploding hand grenade to save his comrades is a classic example of an altruistic suicide. This is considered an act of bravery and self-sacrifice and is generally not even thought of as suicide. For our purposes, there are other types of altruistic suicide we must consider.

Suicide attempts are sometimes used to exact revenge on someone for something they may have said or done. For example, the woman who discovers that her husband has been having an affair might make a suicide attempt as a way of (in her mind) hitting him back.

The adolescent who believes they have been treated unfairly by their parents may attempt suicide to make their parents feel guilty about the "awful" treatment. The young man whose girlfriend broke up with him attempts suicide as a way, albeit in a dysfunctional manner, of showing her how much he loves her and that he cannot go on living without her.

The problem with these (and similar) scenarios is that the person in question did not really want to die. They were simply looking for vengeance or punishment or to send a message.

Another type of altruistic suicide involves someone who sees themselves as a burden. Their suicidal ideation emanates from a belief that their family and friends will be better off without them. This carries a higher level of risk because, unlike the previous scenarios, this person understands the consequences of their actions and expresses an overt desire to die.

Important dynamics come into play here: a lack of self-esteem, poor self-image, an absence of self-worth, and ever-present feelings of worthlessness.

These feelings may stem completely from internalized low self-esteem. These feelings may also be, in part, the result of external factors.

It can be the result of being a target of bullying, a member of a minority group who experiences discrimination, someone harassed on the job. These are just some examples.

Let's also consider why a woman whose husband is cheating on her would choose self-injury to deal with the situation. Or why would a young person attempt suicide to get back at their parents just because they are angry at them?

I have asked these questions in sessions with clients who are expressing these types of thoughts and feelings. I often follow up by asking if they have told their husband or parents how they feel instead of taking their anger out on themselves in a harmful way.

Sometimes, there are reality-based reasons that prevent someone from dealing directly with those who have angered them. For example, a person may be victimized by domestic violence, or an adolescent's parents, though not physically abusive, may be emotionally unavailable and unresponsive to their child's needs. In these cases, confronting the spouse or parent(s) could actually make matters worse.

But why would someone choose to punish themselves for something someone else did? Self-esteem—or lack thereof—is often a major factor.

On occasion, I have literally had to say this to a client: "Do you really think so little of yourself that you are willing to take out your anger and frustration about what someone else did to you on yourself rather than express your feelings to the person who made you feel that way?"

DEALING WITH ANGER

Besides low self-esteem, we must acknowledge anger as the second dynamic at work here. A person expressing suicidal ideation in these circumstances may or may not be depressed, but they are usually angry and simply don't know what to do with their feelings.

As stated above, there may be reality-based reasons for why someone cannot express their anger. Short of that, the intervention strategy in this situation is to help the person understand what they're feeling and learn effective ways to express or deal with their anger in a nondestructive way. Understanding where poor self-esteem enters into the equation is also important. Helping the client develop a more positive opinion of themselves is often a precursor to this process.

There is a story about a therapist who was treating a young adolescent girl that has become somewhat of an urban legend. The client came into a session extremely upset about something that happened between her and her mother, a single parent. The girl said she was very angry and planned to kill herself to get back at her mother.

The therapist suggested an alternative. "Don't kill yourself," she advised. "Go home and bake some cookies." The girl was puzzled.

Her therapist clarified herself. "Bake the cookies at three o'clock in the morning and bang all the pots and pans in the kitchen together and make as much noise as possible."

The girl came into the next session and reported that she had done just as the therapist suggested. The noise from the banging woke her mother, who stormed into the kitchen to see what her daughter was doing.

The girl laughed and shared how she answered her mother. "I'm making cookies!" Apparently, the look on her mother's face was more than enough to make the client feel better.

Oftentimes, the issue isn't about wanting to die. It's about feeling angry and not knowing what to do with it.

This situation could have gone in a much different direction. The clinician's knowledge of the mother-daughter relationship was enough to assure that her suggestion to the daughter was safe. As it turned out, the mother joined in and helped her daughter bake cookies.

We know that there is no cookie-cutter (sorry, pun intended) approach to suicide prevention or any other type of psychotherapeutic strategy. Any approach must be tempered and adapted to a given situation and the person with whom you are working.

Your own training, knowledge, and experience will provide you with the tools you need. Your clients will also let you know what's working and what isn't. Common sense is often your best guide.

PART TWO:

RISK FACTORS AND RED FLAGS

4. DATA AND DEMOGRAPHICS

IF WE WISH to adequately assess someone for suicide risk, several inherent and statistical factors must be considered. One of these factors is demographics, which refers to certain characteristics and their relationship to suicidal risk. That relationship is based on statistical data gathered through various means.

Demographic information is not the only source for determining risk, but it is useful because it allows a provider to partially assess risk based on the cohort in which the client is most categorized.

Some demographic information you acquire will come from the client's basic information that is typically available through intake forms provided by the client or parent. Other more specific demographics will come from your interview with the client and/or family. How you get this information is entirely up to your own style and approach.

As with any assessment, history is important. Developmental, family, peer, school, work, and other related histories will help to put the client's current situation into a broader perspective.

Most of the information regarding risk factors, in this chapter and the next, is based on statistics. Please note, however, that if a person does not fall within one or more of these risk factors, you cannot assume that they are either at low risk or no risk.

For example, if someone falls within a statistically low-risk age group, it does not necessarily mean that you can relax and assume they are not a suicide risk. Obviously, these risk factors are meant to be taken as a whole, and the level of risk should be based partially on your overall evaluation and your assessment of the individual's current mood and functioning.

Statistics are fluid. The risk factors discussed here are based on the most current statistical information available. Statistics can also be geographically biased. Cultural differences and other aspects can influence the numbers. For purposes of this work, the demographic risk factors are based on statistical data here in the United States. The next chapter deals with risk factors related to one's psychological makeup, history of suicidal behaviors, family history, and other items that are more universal, though still geocentric in nature.

AGE

Middle-aged men used to have the highest rates of suicide. The pendulum has swung to an older population. Recent studies identify men over sixty-five as having a higher suicide rate.

In fact, the elderly have the highest increase in suicide rates over the last ten to fifteen years. This growth has outpaced the increase in adolescent suicide in the 1980s, when the rate of suicide among adolescents and young adults under the age of twenty-five more than tripled. The highest rates are among men eighty-five and older.

The rate for adolescents leveled off in the 1990s, but it has not decreased significantly. There was, in fact, a 57 percent increase in suicide rates during 2009 to 2021 for ages fifteen through nineteen. While the rate has leveled off, it has not dropped.

GENDER

Historically, the rate of male suicides has been three times higher than female fatalities. The rate has increased, and recent reports show that men die by suicide at a rate of almost four to one compared to women.

Women, however, attempt suicide three times more often than men. During the 1970s and 1980s, as the women's movement gained momentum and the role of women changed, it was thought that female suicide rates would increase and catch up to, if not surpass, the rates of men.

Many of the "traditional" male roles were, for the first time, being shared by women. There was an assumption (almost a prediction) that the increase in responsibility and inherent stress that came with it would contribute to an increase in the rate of female suicide.

Statistically speaking, an increase in the rate of suicide among women did not occur. There are several contributing factors, but one theory is based on studies showing that when women were subjected to the same level of stress as men, they tended to cope better.

Despite this data, the fact of the matter is this: women do kill themselves.

The other issue is the discrepancy between men and women regarding the methods of suicide attempts. As we know, women tend to attempt suicide three times more often than men. So, why is the difference in the rate of death by suicide influenced by gender? One answer is that men tend to use more violent means of attempting suicide and have a much higher lethality rate.

RACE, ETHNICITY, AND CULTURE

Suicide has historically been referred to as a White man's disease. That notion has changed, and suicide has been considered an "equal opportunity killer" for some time.

While White males were historically the highest group for suicide in terms of racial makeup, no ethnic or racial group is immune. Recent studies show that Native American and White males have the highest rates of suicide. Suicide rates for minority adolescents, especially young Black males, has been on the upswing over the last ten years.

One phenomenon with minimal hard research appears, however, to be very real. It has come to be known as "suicide by cop."

This phenomenon first came to my attention at a conference in Chicago about suicide among adolescents and young adults. One of the presenters was an emergency room physician from Cook County Hospital.

The doctor was open and frank about his experience with this issue. He reported having seen numerous cases of young men who came into the ER after having been shot by a police officer. Many of these gunshot cases were reported to be the result of the young person having pulled out a weapon of their own and pointing it at an officer.

This experience was new to this doctor at the time, as it was for many of us in the audience. These incidents had probably been occurring for much longer than anyone knew. It was only when this doctor and others began to recognize the possible cause for this behavior that they were able to realize how real it was.

Sadly, most of these cases involved young Black men. Many, but not all, were gang related and involved active drug users. Most of these victims led troubled lives and were reported by friends and family to have shown signs of depression.

There are several hypotheses about how and why suicide by cop occurs. There is enough evidence to acknowledge that it is real, and it probably occurs more often than we know.

It is important, however, to differentiate between these types of incidents and other law-enforcement-involved deaths. Even in cases where the alleged perpetrator resists, resulting in their death, one cannot assume it was a case of suicide by cop. The intent of the victim must also be considered when determining cause and effect, and this is not always easy to do.

When it comes to the issue of race and the risk of suicide, we must understand that cultural factors also play a role. Clearly, we cannot say that any one race, ethnicity, or culture is more or less at risk than another. These gross generalizations are misleading and gloss over the roots of the problems.

That said, factors such as race, ethnicity, or culture *do* have an influence. Data regarding race and suicide is important, but risk must be considered within the context of the entire individual, including the factors of age, gender, as well as race, ethnicity, and other factors.

In practice, it is also important to become aware of how your own prejudices, beliefs, and preconceived notions can affect how you react to a client or family. While we must consider the influence that a person's culture may have on them, we should always keep in mind how our own culture and background may influence us.

In addition, consider the fact that there are always individual differences in all of us, regardless of race or culture. These differences must be recognized within the context of the individual, family, and community. We must not lump one person into a set of behaviors, beliefs, or values based solely on their race or ethnicity.

I once participated in a case review of a fourteen-year-old girl who was being considered for foster placement because her father had allegedly sexually abused her. The family was first-generation Italian and very traditional.

One of the participants in the meeting identified himself as having been raised in a similar family constellation. He did not believe that the girl's father was guilty. He explained that he was sure about this because "Italian fathers don't molest their children." Really?

RELIGION

Some religions are clear about where they stand on suicide. For example, I once saw a young adolescent boy who was brought in by his mother because he was having thoughts of suicide. Peter's father had died less than a year prior, and his grieving led to depression.

"How bad does it get, Peter?" I asked.

He teared up. "Pretty bad," he was able to explain between sobs.

As he tried to control himself, his mother spoke up. "He told me he was thinking about killing himself. That scared me. That's when I decided he needed to talk to someone."

I looked at Peter. "Is that true? You think about suicide?"

"I do, sometimes," he admitted.

I went through the checklist in my head and asked some pointed questions. Peter told me he had no specific plan in mind and had not made an actual attempt. Though he was clearly depressed, the thought of him being suicidal seemed incongruous. I cannot explain why I felt that way, but it struck me as out of place. I asked Peter why he wanted to commit suicide.

"If I die," he started to explain, "I can be with my father again. I miss him so much. I thought that if I killed myself, we could be together."

"I understand that, Peter, but you haven't actually made an attempt," I observed. "That's a good thing, and I'm glad you haven't, but I have to ask. What stops you?"

Peter looked at his mother. "She did. She made me not do it."

His mother explained, "We're Catholic. When Peter told me how he was feeling, I took him to see our parish priest. I didn't know what else to do, and it seemed like a good place to start. Father Louis knows us well. He's known Peter since he was a baby. He baptized him and presided over my husband's funeral. So, I took Peter to talk with him. I told Father about what Peter had said, you know, about wanting to kill himself."

I looked over at Peter. "What did Father Louis say to you?"

"He said that suicide was a mortal sin, that if I did kill myself, I wouldn't see my father."

"And did that help?" I asked.

"I think so. I don't think about it as much anymore, but I'm still sad. I still miss my dad." He started crying, and his mother put her arm around him.

"This is why we're here," she said. "It was Father Louis who suggested that we come here. He thought talking with someone would help Peter."

One of the caveats about suicide prevention is that arguing against suicide on religious grounds is generally not considered acceptable or effective. It can even be counterproductive, especially if you don't know how the client and/or family feel about religion.

Like any set of values or beliefs, you must be careful to not impose your own on the client. Fortunately, Peter and his mother's religious beliefs had a positive influence, which I would never negate.

I would, of course, never say to a client in a similar situation that religious beliefs are not an effective argument against committing suicide. If that's what they believe, far be it from me to take that away. Sometimes, suicide prevention must rely on "whatever works."

SEXUAL ORIENTATION

Any teacher knows that they often learn more from their students than their students learn from them. That was certainly the case when I started presenting workshops on suicide. This notion became especially clear when I did a training for a group of high school social workers.

During the question-and-answer period, someone pointed out that I had missed an important factor related to assessing suicide risk for adolescents. When I asked the gentleman to clarify what he was referring to, he said I had not discussed the issue of sexual orientation and gender identity and how it possibly contributes to increased suicidal risk, particularly among LGBTQ+ teenagers.

After hearing that, I felt determined to do research and speak to people in the know about this issue. I soon learned that adolescents struggling with sexual orientation, gender identity, and other related concerns can be and often are at a much higher risk for suicide, sometimes as much as ten times higher. While this issue seems to be a greater risk factor for adolescents, LGBTQ+ adults can also be at a higher risk.

In the last few years, we've seen numerous cases of adolescent suicide where bullying was a large factor and contributed to the young person's feelings of desperation that led them to take their own lives. It is not uncommon for LGBTQ+ adolescents and adults to be targeted and bullied. Social media plays a big part in this issue, which we will cover in a later chapter.

Individuals who identify as gay, lesbian, bisexual, transgender, or queer/questioning their sexual orientation or gender may not only experience bullying; they may also be ostracized by friends, coworkers, the community in which they live, and even their family.

The resulting feelings of alienation and rejection are emotionally painful and can often contribute to intense feelings of depression, leading to suicide. In our current political climate, those feelings can be exacerbated by such legislation that, for example, makes it illegal for the medical community to provide gender-affirming health care.

These external dynamics can affect a person's self-esteem, sense of belonging, and personal validation. Internal dynamics related to this issue must also be recognized. For example, an adolescent who questions their sexual orientation must find a way to cope with their internal struggle and any fear they feel about how others will react to them. Acceptance from peers and family can help to alleviate the potential for self-destructive feelings.

SUBSTANCE USE & ADDICTION

An article in the *Journal of Addictive Diseases* by Norman Miller, Jack Mahler, and Mark Gold states the following:

> The identification of alcohol and drug use and dependence is critical to the proper assessment of suicide. According to studies, over fifty percent of all suicides are associated with alcohol and drug dependence and at least 25 percent of alcoholics and drug addicts commit suicide. Over 70 percent of adolescent suicides may be complicated by drug and alcohol use and dependence. Because alcoholism and drug addiction are leading risk factors for suicidal behavior and suicide, any alcoholic or drug addict should be assessed for suicide, especially if actively using alcohol or drugs.[2]

---

[2]—Miller, N. S., Mahler, J. C., & Gold, M. S. (1991). Suicide Risk Associated with Drug and Alcohol Dependence. Journal of Addictive Diseases, 10(3), 49–61. https://doi.org/10.1300/J069v10n03_06

Alcohol and other depressant drugs increase feelings of hopelessness, which results in an exacerbation of depressive symptoms and raises the level of risk for suicide. Even the nonaddicted person who reports intermittent drug and/or alcohol use needs to be assessed for suicide risk. Alcohol often plays a key role, especially in lethal suicide attempts.

In another study, the following was found:

> The 24-hour period following alcohol intoxication is associated with a seven-fold increase in the risk for suicidal behavior. Moreover, alcohol intoxication is related to greater lethality of attempt methods, making suicide fatalities more likely. Over a third of suicide decedents test positive for alcohol; 63.5% of whom have blood concentrations demonstrating intoxication, and more suicide decedents test positive for alcohol than other substances.[3]

We all do things when we are drunk that we would not do when sober. Drug and alcohol addiction, abuse, or even casual use can and do contribute to one's level of risk.

EXTERNAL FACTORS

A few other potential risk factors are worth noting. Job status is one, especially a recent loss of a job. Case in point, the support group I described earlier. There have also been cases of job changes or even a promotion that created enough stress to become a risk factor.

One's profession or type of employment plays a minor role, but it can contribute. For example, dentists are known to have the highest rates of suicide among professionals, and believe it or not, veterinarians might have a higher rate. Long hours, the stress of dealing with pet

---

3—Mina M. Rizk & Sarah Herzog & Sanjana Dugad & Barbara Stanley Suicide Risk and Addiction: The Impact of Alcohol and Opioid Use Disorders Current Addiction Reports (2021) 8:194–207

owners, and the practice of euthanizing animals have been identified as possible reasons for their enhanced level of risk.

Whatever the person's job, we need to explore what, if any, stressors are associated with it.

Marital status is another. The recent loss of a spouse through death or divorce is a potential source of risk. A single person who never had a significant partner can also be at higher risk.

Geographic location can be a consideration. From a strictly statistical standpoint, more suicides happen west of the Mississippi River than east.

Springtime presents a higher period of risk than other seasons. The so-called holiday blues is somewhat of a myth because suicide rates tend to drop during November and December.

Sunday evenings are a particularly difficult time for anyone feeling depressed or lost. With nothing to look forward to, the notion of facing another week of stress and discouragement can contribute to one's level of risk.

It would be unusual, if not rare, for any one of these factors to be enough to cause someone to commit suicide. Most often, a combination of several factors contributes to one's ideation. Understanding the individual demographics, other factors, and their impact delivers a much more comprehensive risk assessment.

5. A MENTAL STATUS EXAM

NUMEROUS VERSIONS AND formats of a mental status are available. When we conduct a risk assessment, it is important to understand how each component of the exam may or may not impact one's risk for suicide.

Like demographics and behavioral and emotional factors, a client's mental status represents only one part of the picture. For example, if their mental status does not appear to be impaired, they should not automatically be considered low risk for suicide. The same is true for someone whose mental status is impaired in some way. This impression alone does not necessarily mean that the client is a risk for suicide.

MENTAL STATUS EXAM COMPONENTS

» **AFFECT**

Someone who presents with a sad or depressed affect could be considered a suicidal risk, especially if other factors related to their sadness or depression are also present. A flat affect does not necessarily assume a suicidal risk, but it should not be dismissed entirely. Even an agitated affect could be considered a risk factor. It is difficult, if not impossible, to make hard-and-fast statements about each of these, as they are all contextual.

» **ORIENTATION**

A client's orientation to time, place, and circumstance is important when considering risk. Orientation alone does not necessarily put a person at risk. A client can be depressed and suicidal and still be aware of their surroundings, who they are, where they are, the day of the week, etc.

» **VEGETATIVE SIGNS**

Changes in sleep patterns and appetite, with weight gain or loss, are classic physiological symptoms of depression. The presence and intensity of these factors are indicators that can help to determine the seriousness of one's depression and should be considered when evaluating the risk for suicide.

» **IMPULSIVITY**

Many people, especially adolescents, are impulsive by nature. We need to gather specific information about when, where, and how a client may exhibit impulsive behavior. Many suicide attempts, especially but not limited to those made by adolescents, are often made impulsively. This is why we need to explore this factor in detail.

» **INSIGHT**

A person's ability to examine and understand their thoughts, feelings, attitudes, and behavior can be a positive contributor for reducing suicidal risk. It is not enough to accept these understandings on their own because even though someone may thoroughly understand themselves, understanding alone is not usually enough to help a person feel better.

Someone could fully understand their situation and conclude that the only remedy is to commit suicide.

» **JUDGMENT**

Good judgment is a protective factor, particularly in relation to a person's level of impulsivity. When put together, good judgment and insight can often ward off impulsive thoughts that might influence a person to make a suicide attempt.

Each of the components of a mental status exam, when taken together, are an integral part of a comprehensive risk assessment.

6. NEEDLE IN A HAYSTACK

FERRETING OUT INDIVIDUAL factors to determine a level of risk is like finding a needle in a haystack. Many relevant details are not always obvious, and it often takes a great deal of searching on the part of the provider to discover those factors. The items discussed here are meant to provide a road map to help you make those determinations.

PSYCHIATRIC HISTORY

Common sense and our own experience can probably tell us a lot about a client. So, it's easy to say that anyone with a previous history of psychiatric or emotional problems is at a greater risk for suicide than the general population.

Certain factors influence the level of risk for anyone in this category. One of them relates to the person's experience with treatment. Obviously, the more positive experience they have had and the more effective their treatment has been, the less at risk they will probably be for suicide.

We should, however, not assume that a "successful" treatment experience means someone is not at risk. Depending on the type and severity of their disorder, relapse can and often is a real part of a person's experience. This is often the point when risk becomes a greater concern.

FAMILY HISTORY

This is another aspect of risk factors in the realm of psychiatric disorders. For example, a person with a positive family history for clinical depression is at a much higher risk for becoming depressed themselves and, therefore, increases their risk for suicide.

Family histories are often difficult to obtain. The individual client may or may not be aware of his or her family history. It is not unusual for families to try to cover up the fact that old Uncle Joe was just a little bit "crazy."

A family history of substance abuse is also important, but it can be even more difficult to obtain. Substance abuse, particularly alcoholism, has been connected to depression in children of alcoholics. The challenge is to garner a dependable family history.

Let's remind ourselves here that things are not always as they seem. A reliable reporter is often a contradiction in terms. Thankfully, awareness of these issues has recently been on the upswing. Celebrities, sports figures, and others in the public eye have willingly come forward to discuss their struggles and challenges with such things as anxiety and depression. These endeavors should be applauded and encouraged.

That said, I wish we would call it what it is. I recently saw a posting that started with the line "Are you suffering from mental health? If so, we can help." No! We *suffer* from mental *illness*. We *celebrate* our mental health.

OTHER FACTORS TO CONSIDER

» **SUBSTANCE ABUSE HISTORY**

Not every client with a substance abuse history is at risk for suicide. Not every suicidal client has a history of substance abuse. However, a person with a substance abuse history is at a higher risk because they are already engaging in highly risky behavior.

Some overdose deaths are accidental. Some overdose deaths occur "accidentally on purpose." Some overdose deaths are intentional.

An entire body of research exists on what are known as indirect self-destructive behaviors. These actions may not kill someone immediately, but they could result in death.

A history of substance abuse, coupled with other demographic factors such as previous suicide attempts, the presence of depression, poor impulse control, and a lack of insight and judgment, put someone at extremely high risk for suicide.

TREATMENT HISTORY

We need to determine if a client's previous history of mental health treatment or a lack thereof is a risk or protective factor. For example, a client who has never been in treatment may not have felt the need for it because they have always been able to solve their own problems.

It is important to know this information. What aspect of their current circumstance is different, and what has gotten in the way of their ability to resolve it successfully?

If the client has previously been in treatment, you should get as much information about their experiences as possible. Here are some questions to help you do that.

1. What were the circumstances that spurred them to seek treatment?
2. What type of treatment did they receive? Was it inpatient or outpatient?
3. What was the modality? Individual therapy? Family therapy?
4. Has the client ever been on medication? If so, what?
5. Are they currently taking any medication?
6. When did their most recent course of treatment begin, and when, if at all, did it end?
7. Does the client believe that their treatment was helpful?

TRAUMA HISTORY

A client with a history of trauma is at a relatively higher risk for suicide. Survivors of sexual and/or physical abuse, with an accompanying depression and even aggressive behaviors, will often become self-destructive, directly or indirectly.

Former military personnel who are experiencing symptoms of post-traumatic stress disorder will often report having thoughts of suicide, which they consider as a way of ending their inner turmoil. The number of suicides among veterans, especially those who have experienced combat, is at an almost epidemic proportion.

I mentioned Emile Durkheim's work. He described widowhood as a traumatic event. In his work with widows in the traditional culture of turn-of-the-twentieth-century France, he discovered that the first year following the loss of a spouse is crucial.

Whether the same can be said following an emotionally and/or physically traumatic event, such as the death of a loved one, a debilitating accident, or illness, is difficult to say. Any difficulty with adjustment following a trauma can certainly be a contributing factor.

Research is concluding that trauma has a physiological effect on brain development, especially in children and adolescents. It also reveals that trauma appears to have a negative effect in the development of the frontal lobe, where impulsivity and emotion are regulated.

We also see increasing work being conducted on the effects of traumatic brain injury, particularly when it comes to sports injuries. Many cases of suicide by former athletes, especially those who played professional football, are being attributed, at least in part, to the presence of a traumatic brain injury, resulting in a disorder known as chronic traumatic encephalopathy (CTE). We are now seeing more and more publications covering this issue.

RELATIONSHIP STATUS AND SUPPORT SYSTEMS

The presence of positive relationships in one's life can significantly contribute to reducing suicide risk. A strong support system can be utilized in different ways.

The best-case scenario is when a client voluntarily reaches out to a support person for help. However, it is also crucial that the support person responds positively.

A quality support system can play an active role in preventing a vulnerable person from hurting themselves. Most states in the US have laws in place regarding a "duty to warn." This means that if a client is threatening to harm someone—and the provider believes there is imminent risk of harm to that person—the provider must take steps to protect them.

Those steps could include the involuntary hospitalization of the client or notifying law enforcement, the client's family, or the potential victim of the client's intent. Given these circumstances, a provider is protected from lawsuits regarding breach of confidentiality if the provider acted in good faith and believed that the client presented an imminent risk of doing harm to others.

The second part is a "duty to protect." This could apply to those described above, but it can also apply to steps to protect the client from self-harm.

These steps to protect are almost identical to those under duty to warn. The question that is most relevant here is this: How and when do you involve family, friends, partners, etc., to protect the client from self-harm? Given the circumstances, families can and *should* be contacted even if it is against the client's will.

Oftentimes, a provider will work with the family to develop a safety plan, which might involve keeping a close watch on the client. They must also ensure that the client complies with the components of a treatment plan, keeping appointments and taking prescriptions.

All of this assumes that the client has good relationships with family members or those willing to get involved. This is not always the case, and I have seen many clients whose motivation for suicide is partly due to loneliness, having no one to rely on, a breakup, or loss.

This situation comes with its own set of problems. Duty to protect allows for the involvement of police and other entities to provide immediate assistance without the client's consent. This can also include hospitalizing the client against their will. When and how you decide to enlist these resources is a judgment call.

Having no outside support can put a tremendous amount of

pressure on the provider. Rightly or wrongly, a client may come to look at the provider as their only source of support. The client may come to believe that, given their hopelessness and helplessness, it is the provider's sole responsibility to literally keep them alive.

Some practitioners and researchers of crisis intervention theories believe that allowing a certain level of dependency to form between a client and their provider during the early stages of a crisis is acceptable. This is especially true in cases where there is no significant support for the client. That dependency, however, must be weaned over a short period of time while the provider and client work together to help the client develop their own coping abilities.

I have had clients say to me, "You're all I got." I believe it is important in the early stages of treating a client who is at suicidal risk to *not* discount this belief.

Some providers feel it is necessary to respond to a client in this situation by discussing the issue of boundaries and the importance of maintaining a professional relationship. While I agree, I also think there is a fine line between maintaining a position of neutrality and joining with the client in a healthy therapeutic relationship.

Of course, that relationship will change over time, and the process should be one of helping the client develop self-sufficiency and self-soothing. Crisis theory says that meeting those early dependency needs will enable that process to occur more smoothly and in less time.

RECENT LOSS

We discussed the significance of loss in relation to depression and suicide risk. Recent loss is a contributing factor to someone's level of risk, but even a loss that occurred long ago can be a risk factor. A client's reconciliation of that loss can be more important than when it occurred.

The first anniversary of a significant loss may bring up feelings that have not been resolved. It is important to note that even if the client had initially coped well with the loss, certain circumstances might cause associated sadness and grief to resurface.

Birthdays and holidays, such as Thanksgiving, Christmas, and Hanukkah, can also be difficult. This is especially true when it comes to family traditions and rituals.

I try to approach these occurrences in an anticipatory manner. Discussing them with the client *before* the date or event can help them develop coping mechanisms to get through it.

But no matter how hard any of us try, most of us will not be able to avoid some reaction to these significant dates. Grief takes its own time and often creeps in when we least expect it.

I lost both of my parents within a two-week span, and, even though it's been more than twenty years, I still get moody and cranky at that time of year. A good cry still helps. Grief is normal, and we can't fight it.

RECENT SUICIDE OF FAMILY MEMBER, FRIEND, OR CLASSMATE

Losing anyone is difficult. Losing someone to suicide will create grief and loss and possible feelings of guilt and remorse, feelings of having not done enough to prevent the person from dying by suicide. This often becomes a case of the "should-haves."

"I should have paid more attention."

"I should have seen it coming."

"I should have stopped them."

These statements are echoed repeatedly by family members and friends who have lost someone by suicide. Guilt alone may not necessarily drive someone to become suicidal.

Several risk factors that led a person to commit suicide may contribute to a family member's risk. For example, a genetic predisposition for depression.

Suicide as a learned behavior, especially among children and adolescents, is a real risk factor. The so-called contagion effect of suicide among young people is well documented. We have seen several cases of cluster suicides occurring in relatively small communities.

Many experts have attempted to explain this behavior. The most popular version is that these young people were part of a cult or made a suicidal pact with each other.

In most cases, however, the adolescents barely knew each other. The idea of a suicide pact seems to be an attempt for adults to rationalize how and why these events happened.

The more accepted theory is that adolescents are highly suggestible. Someone troubled by depression, hopelessness, and helplessness may believe that, just as they saw another young person find the "answer" to their problems in suicide, they might also be able to do the same.

Here's the bottom line: A death by suicide of a family member or significant other is a risk factor for your client.

PREVIOUS SUICIDE ATTEMPT(S)

Have you ever done something difficult, complicated, challenging, or somewhat risky? Think of something that might fall into at least one of these categories. Try to remember the first time you tried it. What was it like? Was it easy? Difficult? Were you frightened, frustrated, or excited? What did you feel?

Now, think of that same behavior or action that you may have done or experienced more than once. How was it the second time? The third time? The fourth? Did it get easier? Did it become less of a challenge or less scary? Were you more apt to keep doing it?

When I was twelve or thirteen and reckless, we would carry our bikes to the top of the concrete incline below a highway overpass. One such place crossed a sidewalk at the bottom and emptied onto a busy street. The trick was to ride down the hill and either brake hard enough to stop before hitting the street or take a chance and continue across the street without getting hit by a car.

The first time my friends and I tackled this challenge, we did so very slowly, hitting our brakes on and off all the way down. The next time, we took it a little faster.

By the fourth or fifth time, we were bold enough to let ourselves go, consequences be damned. Thankfully, no one got hurt, but needless to say, we were foolish.

If you think of the dynamics and behavior associated with a suicide attempt and relate it back to an experience you may have had (such as my example), it will help you understand one of the reasons why a person with a previous history of suicide attempts is at a much higher risk.

Statistically speaking, most people who die by suicide had a history of two prior attempts. Most people with a history of prior suicide attempts initially choose a method with a relatively low risk of lethality and gradually "move up" to a method that is highly lethal.

Few who make an initial attempt by a gunshot will later make a subsequent attempt with an overdose, although there are cases of people surviving gunshot wounds even to the head.

It is important to gather this kind of information from a client, family member, or *reliable* source to report a client's history of suicide attempts. Do not be lulled into thinking that no prior attempts mean you can relax and assume zero risk. Risk must be assessed on a continuum.

Like any other risk factor, you must be willing to ask about previous attempts. Risk factors can be identified in several ways. Some are based on age, race, etc., while others can only be assessed through open discussion.

WHAT'S THE POINT?

So, what do you do with all this information? Taking each of the demographic, familial, and historical factors into consideration is one part of a comprehensive risk assessment. To understand how this information can be helpful, let's put it all together.

From a strictly statistical standpoint, the most suicidal person is a White older male. He lives alone, works in a "white-collar" capacity, lives west of the Mississippi River, and has experienced a significant loss in the past six months. This person has a history of two prior suicide attempts and has no support systems. He has a plan in mind and the means to carry it out. He is alone on a Sunday evening in late spring.

How does knowing this composite profile help?

I was the after-hours on-call person for the same crisis program I discussed earlier. Sure enough, around 7:30 p.m. on a Sunday in mid-May, I received a crisis call from a sixty-something-year-old widow who said she was going to kill herself.

The caller explained that she had just had a fight with her two adult children. They got into a shouting match that resulted in her throwing (and breaking) every dish she owned at her children. Her kids stormed out of the house, swearing to never return. She had a package of razor blades, and if someone did not do something, she was going to cut her wrists.

Thankfully, this caller was cooperative and wanted help, so we talked for a while. After gaining her trust, I suggested we get her to the local hospital emergency department for an evaluation. She agreed, and I arranged for a medical transport car.

Besides the fact that this caller was female and lived just east of the Mississippi, she was the most statistically at-risk person I had ever encountered. Knowing the risk factors and being able to apply them helped me develop a clearer picture of what I was facing. I also didn't need to go into her history. Her presentation was more than enough.

Before diving into more factors in risk assessment, let's discuss two important cohorts.

7. SPECIFIC POPULATIONS

THERE ARE NUMEROUS ways to identify and define a specific population. There is also a great deal of expertise necessary to adequately address the needs of each.

My intent here is to address the concerns and needs of those groups about which I believe I am most familiar. There are other experts, such as those who work with at-risk veterans, whom I would suggest you seek out and learn from.

ADOLESCENTS

The first chapter of John Meeks's book about adolescent psychotherapy, *The Fragile Alliance*, is called "Adolescents Are Different." Those three words capture the essence of what we need to understand about young people.

GENERAL CHARACTERISTICS

Adolescents share certain characteristics in varying degrees, some of which serve them well, while others put them at risk for an assortment of negative consequences.

Adolescents are impulsive. The level of impulsivity varies from person to person and generally tempers as one gets older. This is an important factor in determining suicide risk among adolescents and makes predicting suicidal risk more difficult.

Adolescents are "bipolar" by nature. Hormonal changes, growth spurts, and rapid physiological changes all contribute to what seems to be a constant condition of mood swings.

Your teenage daughter or son may storm into the house after school, stamp their feet on their way to their room, slam the door shut, and crank up the volume or plug in their earbuds to hear some sad, bitter, or angry music. Five minutes later, that same young person may come downstairs, give you a smile and, if you're lucky, maybe even a hug, and say, "What's for dinner?"

Adolescents are moody. I use this term loosely and somewhat tongue-in-cheek because there is a certain normalcy to these changes in mood.

Feelings of sadness and discouragement are a somewhat normal part of the adolescent developmental process. It is important to monitor these feelings, especially if the adolescent develops more intense feelings of depression and despair. Most young people get discouraged at one time or another, but they are usually able to work through those feelings.

My rule of thumb is three to five days. If the young person continues to show signs of depression beyond that period, my antenna goes up, and I start thinking about how I might intervene. This does not mean I ignore those feelings during the first three to five days. It means that after a certain time, my flag goes from yellow to red.

Early adolescence is accompanied by great change and adjustment. This stage can also include periods of self-doubt, low self-esteem, and a general feeling of self-loathing.

Not every adolescent who experiences these feelings is going to become suicidal. These uncertainties related to one's self-esteem can become more intense and might exacerbate a mild sense of sadness or depression and turn it into something more serious.

Adolescents tend to over-awfulize. This means that what may seem like a somewhat minor problem or concern to adults may feel like an overwhelmingly devastating situation to a young person.

PERSPECTIVE IS KEY

I once had a high school senior referred to me due to signs of depression and ongoing expressions of desperation. There was no family history of depression and no predisposition or precipitant that her parents could identify. I was a bit taken aback when I asked the client what she thought the source was for these feelings.

This young woman attended a high school in an upper-middle-class suburban community. She reported that, due to circumstances at home, she was going to have to ride the school bus to and from school. She clearly identified this as the source of her depression. When I asked her to clarify this for me, she simply stated, "Seniors don't ride the bus!"

Perception is nine-tenths of reality, and for this person, the prospect of having to ride the bus was demeaning. What's more, the fear of being seen by her friends and classmates was more than enough to trigger her feelings.

Was this client at risk for suicide? Nothing pointed to that, but I mention this case as an example of how we need to look at things from the perspective of the client. This is especially true when working with adolescents.

TIME IS RELATIVE

Another phenomenon of adolescence is that they experience time differently than adults.

We all have an internal time clock, which gives us a sense of the passage of time. Our internal clocks also regulate our schedule. This is why, even though on a holiday, we still manage to wake up at 6 a.m., the same as on a regular workday.

As we get older, time seems to move faster. I am certainly finding that to be the case.

For children and adolescents, time moves slower. Tell a child they may have to wait a week for something, and you might as well be talking about a month or a year.

Walk into any high school or middle school during the last class period on a Friday, and you will see another example of this phenomenon. To the kids in that class, time seems to stop. Those last forty-five minutes of the school day and the week slow down to a crawl. It feels like it takes hours for the school day to finally end.

This concept is important when it comes to suicide prevention with children and adolescents. First, for an adolescent, feelings of desperation, hopelessness, helplessness, and worthlessness can set in very quickly and may seem to last forever.

I have interviewed several young people over the years who report feelings of depression and an accompanying sense of hopelessness and despair. When asked how long they have been feeling that way, they often respond, "Since yesterday." While this may surprise the adult in the room, for an adolescent, "yesterday" was long ago.

Second, an adolescent's perception of time will have an impact on how you present the amount of time it will probably take for them to get better. Three to six months seems like a lifetime to a young person.

It becomes incumbent on you to develop a timeline that describes the process in shorter steps. A week is usually a reasonable length of time, but in some cases, even taking it day by day may be necessary.

UNDER THE INFLUENCE

Adolescents are suggestible and quick to imitate the behavior of others. This is one of the theories behind the explanation for the cluster suicides among adolescents we saw in the 1980s.

In some instances, suicide is considered a learned behavior. A young person struggling with their own feelings of depression and hopelessness may learn of another adolescent who committed suicide. In their mind, they may start to believe that perhaps that other person found suicide as the answer and that maybe they could follow in their footsteps.

This is why, when the suicide of a young person becomes public through the media or other outlets, it is crucial to also convey a message that suicide is *not* the answer and that this is *not* an acceptable behavior.

LOGICAL CONSEQUENCES

Adolescents believe they are invincible. Young people do not always equate suicide with dying. They see it as a way of manipulating others around them, exacting revenge on someone who had wronged them, or calling attention to themselves and the fact that they have a problem.

One young person told me he was going to go home over the weekend and commit suicide and then go to school on Monday to see the reaction of friends and fellow students.

Clearly, this adolescent did not understand or wish to acknowledge the possible consequences of his behavior. My intervention was simple. I took out a piece of paper and literally wrote out an equation and handed it to my client: "Suicide = Dead."

The logical consequence of this young man's committing suicide was that he was going to die. In his mind, however, it had a totally different outcome.

We talked about death and what that means. After a while, he began to admit that he really did not want to die. Once he realized that, we explored his feelings that led him to this point and how he could deal with them more effectively.

Understanding the meaning of death and appreciating it as a possible outcome of a suicide attempt can be an effective intervention with adults too.

SEE ME!

Suicide is often used as an attention-getting device. This is especially true with adolescents. It is difficult for a young person to approach someone, whether a parent or someone else, and admit directly that they are experiencing feelings of depression or cannot overcome a problem they are having and need to speak to someone. It rarely happens that way.

Here's the problem. It's sometimes easy for adults to dismiss a young person's suicidal feelings by saying that they really don't mean it and are only saying such a thing to get attention.

I have two responses to that kind of statement. The first is to try to explain that young people do a lot of things for attention, both positively and negatively.

In some cases, after a careful assessment, I might agree with the parents that their child *is* threatening suicide as an attention-getting device. I then ask the parents if they are willing to risk their child's life with this assumption.

My second approach is simple. I look at them and say, "So, pay attention!"

Many people, not just adolescents, die as the result of a suicide attempt that was meant only as a cry for attention.

Norman Farberow and Edwin Shneideman titled their first book *The Cry for Help*. They saw suicide as not only a wish to die but as a way for a depressed person to communicate their need for help when they are not able to come right out and ask for assistance.

It is difficult for most of us, much less a person experiencing depression and possible suicidal ideation, to ask for help. Suicide becomes a mechanism to display their feelings.

A young man was referred to me after he exhibited a series of negative behaviors. He ran away. He broke curfew. He came home drunk. He cut school and was barely passing most of his classes. The school decided he needed help.

As I explored these behaviors during the initial interview, this young man suddenly broke down and started crying. After he regained composure, he told me he was glad I was talking to him. "No one wants to listen to me," he said.

"Listen to you about what?" I asked.

He started to sob again. "About me. About how I feel."

"So, tell me, how do you feel?"

"I don't know. I'm not right. I don't feel right."

"You've been acting out quite a bit," I pointed out. "Is that what you're talking about?"

He hung his head. "Not really. I mean, maybe. I just feel like something's wrong, and no one will listen. I know I do all these things, and I get in trouble, but no one listens."

"No one listens. Who doesn't listen?"

"My parents don't get it. They think I'm just a bad kid. They don't understand."

"Tell me. What don't they get?" I explored. "What don't they understand?"

He frowned. "They don't get it. I'm not a bad kid. I just do these things, and they ignore me."

He finally looked up at me. "I mean, how far do I have to go? What do I have to do to get them to realize that I have a problem? Do I have to kill myself? Will they listen to me then?"

We need to understand our client's suicidal ideation from a risk perspective, but we also need to understand how and why they might be using this behavior as communication. Considering this case, empathy and understanding could go a long way.

The other dynamic to understand, which I often discuss with parents, is *why* their child has chosen suicide as their way of coping with a situation or problem. This is especially crucial in situations where the parents may not take their child's ideation seriously.

In those cases, I try to explain that adolescents choose many ways to act out. These behaviors may occur out of spite or as a coping mechanism, dysfunctional though they may be.

Adolescents may choose to run away, drink, abuse drugs, or be sexually active.

Suicidal ideation can be an unconscious or conscious choice that an adolescent makes. Regardless of the circumstance, this ideation must be taken seriously. If I'm proven wrong and overreacting, so be it, but if there is something going on that speaks to the need for attention, we need to respond in a way that is helpful and supportive of the child.

PAY ATTENTION!

Adolescents do not have the market cornered on these behaviors. Adults also make suicide threats to get attention. Desperation and hopelessness may set in quickly and they may exhibit some of the same dynamics as adolescents.

We must take any threat seriously, no matter how minimal it may seem. Let the person in question know you take them seriously. This validates their feelings and demonstrates your willingness to listen as you offer any assistance they may require.

Next, especially with adolescents, reinforce the notion of the potential finality of their decision. Let them know that no matter how bad things may appear, they *can* get better. Remember the operant term is *can*, not *will*. Then, offer to, in effect, join them in figuring out how to make things better.

Make it a "we" thing.

SPECIAL POPULATIONS: THE "CHRONICALLY" SUICIDAL CLIENT

Anyone working in a helping profession has encountered a "chronically" suicidal client. Those of us who have worked in crisis centers have seen them often: a client who repeatedly refers to or threatens to commit suicide with no history of any attempts. The threats can be veiled and difficult to discern, while some are more obvious.

Another subgroup of clients may make suicide attempts, but the method they use has a low risk of lethality. Others choose a higher-risk method but always build in a rescue scenario.

These can be frustrating situations for the provider and the client's family and friends. The provider's frustration centers around the fact that these threats or attempts must be taken seriously and handled the same way as any other client who presents with suicidal ideation.

Even though you know, based on a long history with this client, that they will probably not make an attempt, or at least not a serious one, you cannot take the chance.

Family members often find themselves in the same position. At times, they reach a point where their frustration is so great that they are almost ready to give up on the person. I have often heard family members say, "I almost wish they would do it and just get it over with."

Most family members don't really believe that. If they did, we would have a whole other set of problems to address. Usually, what motivates a statement like that is a family that simply doesn't know what else to do because they feel like they have given as much support as they can.

For providers, the issue is complicated by the legal and ethical standards we must adhere to, along with our standards of practice and beliefs that all clients have worth.

THE PERILS OF MANIPULATION

When I do my suicide prevention training, this issue often generates a lot of discussion. During one session, a participant described suicide as the ultimate manipulation. We talked about how this is often the case, but it is also a circumstance that we cannot ignore or pass off simply as the client's attempt to be manipulative.

There is an extensive history of clients who use suicide as a manipulative device and have died as the result. We've seen numerous cases of people who have made suicide attempts knowing that their method is not lethal or someone will intervene to ensure their survival.

Unfortunately, there are always unknown variables that can come into play, and the result may be death. This is one reason why we cannot ignore any threat of suicide.

There are ways to address this issue. The biggest obstacle is that the client must be willing to go down that road with you. Consciously or not, the client often sees their behavior as serving a useful purpose for them. So, if that is the case, why would they want to give it up?

The other obstacle is that many of our clients are often unwilling to participate in follow-up services. There is a sort of crisis mentality that is shared by many people.

This is also why the percentage of people who do follow through and participate in ongoing services is often low.

PROBING FOR DETAILS

First, process together the details of the client's most recent suicidal ideation or attempt. Ask, "What brought you to this point? What was your motivation? What impact were you hoping to have on others?" This will help you understand their cognitive and emotional state.

There is a secondary gain here. By asking these questions (and others), you bring the client's thoughts and feelings into their conscious awareness, which may provide useful information. You also want to find out if a client's expressed suicidal ideation or attempt was based on a real wish to die. While this can be a tricky question and can open doors a client may not be ready to enter, it needs to be addressed.

Once you have established a client's motivation, start to discuss the problems or concerns that led them to that point. Some clients will be open about their issues while others may struggle to identify what led them to threaten or attempt suicide. For some clients, the behavior becomes an automatic response to stressful or difficult situations.

YOUR ROLE AS PRACTITIONER

First, help your client become aware of the impact of their behavior on themselves and those around them. In rare circumstances, I have brought in members of a client's family and allowed them to discuss the impact of the client's behavior on them.

This takes a bit of coaching because I never want the family to gang up on the client, which could only add guilt to the equation. On one level, suicide is deeply personal, but it also affects others in different ways, so I want to be sure that the family can be caring and supportive.

Second, assuming you can help a client overcome their suicidal ideation, your next step is to help them identify what keeps leading them to becoming suicidal.

Third, help your client develop new coping skills and more effective ways of dealing with these problems and concerns.

How you get there depends on multiple factors: your client, their circumstances, your training and experience, the setting where you practice, and other variables. Even choosing a modality depends on circumstances. Whether you work with a client individually, in family therapy, or within another group setting can influence the outcome.

No matter what type of situation you are in, it can be frustrating for you as a provider and for your client's family and friends. That said, if anyone ignores the problem, it will not simply go away. It is your job as a practitioner to keep everyone engaged.

PART THREE:

TOM'S SUICIDE ASSESSMENT TOOL

8. ARE YOU FEELING SUICIDAL?

OVER THE PAST few years, I have seen an increase in the number of suicide assessment tools. Some have catchy names. Others just use acronyms. This section presents a different approach to risk assessment.

Having looked at several assessment tools and discussed them with many people trained in their use, I can conclude that, for the most part, there isn't much difference between them. Risk factors are basically the same. Despite any different labels or approaches, the process of assessing risk is basically the same in each of these models.

Most of the assessment tools I have reviewed focus primarily on content and include symptoms, reasons behind suicidal ideation, previous history, support systems, etc.

My approach is different. Certainly, I look at the factors that I've mentioned, but I also examine the process related to one's ideation. I want to know things like the onset and duration of the ideation, the intensity of the feelings, and how the person experiences them.

Please understand that I cannot provide a script. I cannot give you specific words to use in doing a suicide assessment. I *can* give you direction.

I will outline what information is important to gather, but how you collect that information should be based on your own style and approach.

As I mentioned, when I do a risk assessment, I look at it from two perspectives: content and process. In some ways, I believe process is even more important than content. We'll review this next, but first, there is an important issue that needs consideration.

THE BIG ASK

Of course, the risk factors and demographics are an important part of your overall risk assessment. The information you get during your interview with a client, along with taking note of factors like age and gender, will all contribute to your assessment, but there is a precursor that needs to be addressed. You have to ask the question!

How you approach the subject is entirely up to you, and there are several ways of doing so, depending on your comfort level, your client's, and possibly their family. Some lessons, however, are learned the hard way, and I came to realize during my first-year graduate internship that the direct approach is often best.

I was conducting an initial interview with a young man who presented with symptoms of depression and anxiety. After reviewing his concerns and history, I knew I would have to approach the question of whether he was having thoughts of suicide.

While still not completely comfortable with my own feelings and not wanting to alarm the client, I tried to address the issue in what turned out to be a very clumsy fashion. I asked him whether he was having any thoughts of "doing something."

The client looked puzzled. "I don't understand," he said.

I tried again. "You know, thinking about doing something," I asked again.

It was obvious from his expression that he still did not understand my question. Finally, I took another crack at it. "Have you been having thoughts of suicide?" I asked.

He gave a somewhat forced smile. "Oh, yes. Yes, I have," he answered.

He looked almost relieved that I had finally addressed the issue directly. We went on to explore his ideation, the factors behind it, and his current level of risk.

The lesson was to not hedge and don't ease my way into the topic by using a euphemism. The lesson for you is that to do an effective assessment, you must be willing to ask the question.

There will be times when a client will openly report to you that they have been having thoughts of suicide. This is especially and obviously true in cases where depression and suicide are the client's presenting problems. Other times, the issue will not be as apparent but will still need to be addressed as part of your overall evaluation of the client.

Timing is everything, and that phrase has never carried more meaning than in the field of mental health and human services. What you say to a client is important. How you say it matters. But *when* you say it is also important.

In my experience, the "opportunity" to discuss the issue of suicide presents itself in three ways.

The first and most obvious is the client who comes to see you when the presenting problem is recent and/or has persistent thoughts of suicide. In many respects, this makes your job much easier because the client is already coming to you with specific concerns related to suicide.

The second, more common scenario is the client who presents with issues and concerns that may, in your professional opinion, cause you to believe that this person is at risk. For example, a client may report feelings of depression and anxiety and may also, based on information you gather from the client, have other emotional and psychological factors and demographic characteristics that contribute to their level of risk.

In this second scenario, the client may be open about their thoughts and feelings but may not report suicidal ideation. Despite this, you might have reason to believe they are at risk.

My approach would be to first provide feedback to the client and/or family of what I understand to be their problem, concerns, and accompanying feelings and symptoms. I would also say that, given the information they have provided, it is not unusual for someone in such a situation to have thoughts of suicide. I would then ask, "Is this the case?"

This approach can accomplish several things. First, it enables me to communicate that I have a good understanding of the client's problem and how they are feeling. It can also indicate that I understand their problem and have been down this road before.

Last, by bringing up the subject of suicide, I help to begin a discussion about a topic that is often scary for the client to mention.

The third circumstance is the client who presents to you with no current or previous suicidal ideation, no history of suicide attempts, and a presenting problem that appears to have no possible connection whatsoever to any of the known risk factors for suicide. When this is the case, you might ask why you would assess this client for suicide risk.

The simple answer is that I assess everyone for suicidal risk, whether it appears to be relevant to their situation or not. I do this for two reasons.

One, I want to be thorough in my assessment and document the client's response to my questions regarding suicide. Am I also covering myself by doing this? Absolutely!

More importantly, I want to bring the issue into the client's and/or family's awareness, communicating that suicide and ideation can present even in unrelated circumstances.

My second reason is based on experience. Many times, I have sat with a family who presented with a stated problem that seems unrelated to suicidal concerns. When I ask the child about suicide, however, I have been told that they have either thought about or attempted suicide.

While that type of response does not surprise me anymore, I am still amazed at how often the parents' eyes get big, and their jaws drop. These parents had no idea.

The point is this: Be willing and able to ask the question. Make it part of your initial assessment. If someone is put off, that's fine. Acknowledge their offense and explain that this is part of your regular assessment. Being put off also tells you something about their level of risk.

Understanding there are exceptions to every rule, someone who is startled or offended by the question is probably at a relatively low risk.

For others, it may open a door to talk about their thoughts and feelings, especially those that are too scary and painful to bring up on their own.

APPROACHES FOR THOSE WHO ADMIT TO BEING SUICIDAL

Here is the first question:

» **ARE YOU FEELING SUICIDAL?**

You've probably heard the myth. If we ask this question of someone who is not suicidal, we will have planted the idea in their head, and as a result, they will attempt suicide. This is simply not true. Asking the question actually opens the door to discuss persistent feelings.

If the client answers in the affirmative, and I find that most people are generally honest, there is more information to gather. That does not necessarily mean you go down a checklist and ask these questions in the way they are written.

You must develop your own style and approach to get this information in a way that is comfortable for you and your client. As practitioners, we must tailor our style, techniques, and approaches based on the presenting problem, current level of functioning, and needs of our clients. We must adapt to the situation and the needs of the client. I point this out to remind you that the information I am providing is meant as a guide and not a script.

When assessing risk, pay attention to process as much as content. Yes, I want to know more about what the person is thinking and feeling. I also want to know what those experiences are like for them. As you go through the questions below, this will begin to make more sense.

These questions, presented in a somewhat logical order, will enable you to get the information that is important to complete an effective assessment of suicidal risk.

» **HOW LONG HAVE YOU BEEN FEELING SUICIDAL?**

The longer a person has been feelings suicidal, the higher the risk. This is not to say that someone who has been experiencing these feelings for a brief time is not, or could not, be at just as high a risk as someone who has been having these feelings over a longer time.

It's difficult to generalize, but from my own experience, clients who have been experiencing suicidal feelings longer also tend to have experienced increased feelings of hopelessness and helplessness as a precursor to their ideation.

Suicidal ideation of a more recent onset and shorter duration can be just as serious. Either way, the intensity of the ideation is an important factor.

» **ARE THE FEELINGS CONSTANT, OR DO THEY COME AND GO?**

Suicidal feelings that are more intermittent in nature pose less risk than someone whose feelings are more constant.

Suicidal ideation that comes and goes may allow me to intervene and make headway with a client during periods when they are not feeling suicidal and feeling more hopeful.

Persistent ideation presents a different level of risk and a more difficult challenge for the provider. The client who ruminates about suicide is generally more resistant to any suggestions of alternative ways of dealing with their depression.

» **HOW DO YOU FEEL ABOUT THOSE FEELINGS?**

This is a complicated question, and I often find people are confused by it. What I am looking for here is how their suicidal thoughts and feelings are affecting them. In other words, are they comfortable with those thoughts and feelings, and does the idea of killing themselves feel as though that might be the answer?

If that is the response to the question, I am concerned because it increases their level of risk. Having suicidal thoughts and feelings puts a person at a certain level of risk, but being comfortable with those feelings and considering suicide as the possible answer to their problems complicates the issue even more and makes a successful intervention more difficult.

On the other hand, when a person reports that they are frightened by their suicidal thoughts or feelings, I tend to assess them as being at a relatively lower risk. Since everything is relative, when I say lower risk, I am not saying they are at *no* risk.

People can have thoughts and feelings about hurting themselves, a.k.a. self-injurious behaviors, or taking their own lives without ever acting upon those thoughts and feelings. I have often met clients who report having suicidal ideation but are honest in their belief that they would never act on those feelings. Many people understand that while they may have those thoughts and feelings, acting on them is not a choice they would make.

These are the clients who pose less of a threat to themselves. They are also easier to work with, in that they understand and believe that suicide is not the answer. Your role is to reinforce this belief and help the client find alternative ways of dealing with their problems or concerns.

Often, the client may not see suicide as the answer, but they may also not see any other alternative. This is partially a function of depression, and, more importantly, a function of the hopelessness that people who feel suicidal often experience. Tunnel vision is likely also at work.

The intervention strategy is to reassure the person that there are alternatives and that you will work with them to discover what those are. Keep in mind that it is not your job to offer specific alternatives or solutions to the client's problems. Your role is to help them find them.

The question of how they feel regarding suicidal ideation is process-oriented. First, it gives you some idea of the client's comfort level in relation to their suicidal feelings.

Second, their response will set the stage for how and at what level you need to intervene.

» **HAVE YOU TOLD ANYONE ELSE ABOUT THESE FEELINGS?**

Whether a person has communicated their suicidal feelings

to anyone else is important. It is true that most individuals who make a suicide attempt will have conveyed warning signs, some are more overt than others. However, one's ideation is not often communicated directly.

Anyone who does not communicate chooses that route for various reasons. Some clients tell me they did not want to tell anyone for fear that they might try to stop them. These individuals are obviously at high risk.

Other clients fear that they may not be taken seriously or might be ridiculed. Some have tried to communicate their feelings in the past but didn't get the response they were hoping for, and that made them feel worse.

The reason for concealing their feelings does not matter. What's most important is that by not communicating, the client has closed the door to help, and by doing so, they consciously or unconsciously reinforce those feelings of hopelessness and, more prominently, worthlessness.

"I have not told anyone how I feel because I don't matter to them."

"They are better off without me anyway."

"No one would care even if I did tell them."

"They were right about me all along."

These are a sampling of the myriad reasons I have heard over the years. In these situations, an interesting dynamic occurs during my session with them. There will usually come a point, during my initial interview, where a here-and-now experience occurs. This is when I point out, "You do realize that you just did tell me about your suicidal feelings."

Some clients might consider my observation to be intrusive. Some may decide to close up or end the session. In a few cases, the person leaves and does not return. Depending on the level of risk, I may have to consider exercising my duty to warn/protect and notify the family.

So much of how and when to use this type of intervention depends on your relationship with the client. This is, of course, more difficult with a new client, where the relationship has yet to be developed. Sometimes, it's enough to note in my head that the client disclosed it to me and leave it at that. This depends on the level of risk. Most often, there is a need for some sort of intervention.

Most clients are encouraged to know that they disclosed their feelings and that it didn't scare me or cause me to dismiss their feelings or reject them. If anything, it creates an environment that helps the client feel more comfortable discussing any uncomfortable feelings.

You can often see it in their reaction, the heavy sigh of relief when they realize that someone cared enough to want to know how they are feeling. It can be a visible physical reaction, and you can almost see the tension leave their body, often with tears, not so much from pain but from relief. All of these are signs that a client can finally discuss what's really going on.

While it is important to understand the whys of clients who choose not to communicate their suicidal feelings, the reality is that most people do disclose their feelings in some way. The answer of how someone opens up about their suicidal ideation is multidimensional. Clients often report having told a spouse, parent, friend, or teacher, in person or by telephone, text, or note.

The information age and social media has changed all of that. Someone may still communicate their ideation directly to someone; however, there are countless examples of individuals who posted their feelings online, sometimes even about their plan to commit suicide. Often, these and other methods of communication are met with skepticism, disbelief, and even scorn.

Even if someone communicates their feelings to a family member or friend, most people have no idea how to respond. Most often, the lack of an effective response is not necessarily due to indifference or lack of caring. Generally, the person is simply not trained or prepared.

Like most components of an assessment, one question often leads to another. If a client reports that they have communicated to someone, then I want specific information. Who did they tell? How did they communicate? How direct were they? In other words, did they come right out and say they were going to kill themselves, or did they make vague references to their feelings?

Again, process is as important as content. While I want to know what they said, I also want to know what mechanisms and processes they used to communicate their feelings.

As we follow a logical progression in the assessment process, here's the next question.

» **IF YOU DID TELL SOMEONE, WHAT KIND OF RESPONSE DID YOU RECEIVE?**

Since we have so many channels of communication, it is important to know what means were used. Online platforms are far less personal than direct communication with a real person. Any responses that the client receives tend to be less personal and could come from anyone.

The sad reality of social media is that not every response to an online posting is positive or encouraging. Sometimes, they have little to do with the original post and become a forum for people to air their irrelevant issues.

Texting and emails tend to be a little more direct and personal, but they often lack the appropriate emotional context. A response that might include a sad emoji is of little help.

It is important to know that, if the client shared their feelings with someone, I want to get as much detail as possible about how that message was conveyed. Once that is accomplished, I want to know what kind of response they received.

Most people will respond to someone's sharing of their suicidal thoughts in specific ways. One of the most common responses is "You shouldn't talk that way." Another is "You don't really mean that." There are more common responses, ranging from "Don't be silly!" to "Are you crazy?" and none of these can be interpreted as helpful or supportive.

It is unfair to say that any of these negative responses to someone feeling suicidal will cause them to make a suicide attempt, but these responses do little to lower a person's risk.

Anyone who communicates their suicidal feelings to someone that they feel might be able to help is more likely looking for a response of care and concern. "What can I do to help?" is what a suicidal individual wants and needs to hear.

While there is no definitive evidence that a caring response will lower the risk, there is enough evidence on an empirical level to suggest that it will at least not increase their risk.

» **HAVE YOU THOUGHT ABOUT HOW YOU WOULD KILL YOURSELF?**

This is an important question to ask for two basic reasons. First, the more specific a person is regarding the method they have chosen for committing suicide, the more they are at risk. Second, the more lethal the means, the higher the chances that their attempt will result in death.

A person who reports having suicidal thoughts and feelings who has not come up with a specific plan to kill themselves is at less risk, relatively speaking, than a person who reports that when they leave your office, they are going to go home and shoot themselves in the head. This alone, however, does not indicate which person may be more or less liable to attempt suicide.

Certainly, the method that the person has chosen will indicate a person's potential to die from their suicide attempt. This will also impact how you choose to intervene. We must also keep in mind that the intent behind a person's chosen method is just as important in relation to their suicide risk as the potential lethality of the method they have chosen.

I know of a case of a young woman whose suicide attempt was to take three aspirin. Barring any unforeseen circumstances, three aspirin is not enough to kill most people and would cause little distress to the average person. However, growing up, she was warned repeatedly by her mother to never take three aspirin and that doing so could kill a person.

This belief led this woman to take four aspirin as a means of committing suicide.

This is a clear example of how and why intent is just as important as means. Providing adequate intervention should be based on more than one factor. This young woman's level of risk was just as high as someone who had a plan to kill themselves by gunshot.

» **DO YOU HAVE THE MEANS AVAILABLE?**

Anyone in law enforcement, especially those who investigate homicides, will tell you there are three major factors to consider in determining the who, when, where, how, and why of a murder case: motive, method, and means. They can also be applied when assessing suicidal risk.

We have already discussed the primary motives for wanting to commit suicide and the importance of determining the method a person has chosen.

The last is based on the person's chosen method. Do they have the stated means available to carry out their plan? For example, if a client reports that their plan is to shoot themselves in the head, ask these questions: Do you have access to a gun? Do you own a gun? If not, do you know where and how to gain access to a firearm?

Having the means to go through with their plan is the single most important factor in relation to immediacy and intervention. A person who has verbalized suicidal ideation, accompanied by a specific plan but without means to carry out their plan, is at a relatively lower risk than someone who does have the means available to them.

As much as I dislike rating scales, it might be helpful to think about suicide risk in those terms. On a scale of one to ten, a person who expresses suicidal ideation but has no specific plan and no means available is probably around three or four. Someone who expresses suicidal ideation with a specific plan would score around five to seven, depending on the potential lethality of the method they have chosen. Someone expressing suicidal ideation with a specific plan and the means to carry out that plan would probably score between eight and ten, depending on the potential lethality of the method they have chosen.

These are unscientific guidelines. There are no hard-and-fast rules. I know of clients who I would have initially assessed as being at moderate risk but made a serious, and, in one case, lethal suicide attempt. Every situation is relative, and once again, one size does *not* fit all.

» **WHAT DO YOU THINK KILLING YOURSELF WILL ACCOMPLISH, AND DO YOU UNDERSTAND THE POTENTIAL CONSEQUENCES OF THIS ACTION?**

I put these two questions together because they are so related. The first part is an attempt to examine what the person hopes the outcome will be from their suicide attempt.

A person who believes that killing themselves will put an end to their pain and make all their problems go away forever is at a high level of risk. The person who says that committing suicide will cause others, be it family, friends, a teacher, a boss, etc., to feel sad and guilty is still at a relatively high level of risk but may be more workable.

Determining with your client what their goal is will give you greater insight into the problems and issues that led them to this point and what you can do to help them find alternatives (other than suicide) to deal with their issues.

For example, someone who wants the pain of depression to go away can often do so with your help through psychotherapy and perhaps a regimen of antidepressant medication, when indicated. The caveat here is that this process takes time. Depending on the situation, you may still have to take more immediate steps to address their ideation.

Someone who believes that their suicide will cause sadness and guilt in others is often using that to express their anger and frustration with the person or persons who have "wronged" them to such an extreme that they believe they, themselves, must also take extreme measures. Often, the issue is not depression or a wish to die. It is more a desire to get back at the people who treated the suicidal individual so badly.

On a strictly logical and well-informed level, the second part of this question regarding consequences of their suicidal action may seem unnecessary to ask. However, not everyone who makes a suicide attempt understands that they might die because of that attempt.

This is particularly true among adolescents, especially those who are vulnerable to the "magical thinking" that typically goes on in the brains of young people. They feel as though they are invincible and that nothing can hurt them.

There is also a certain "not me" attitude, a thought process based on the false assumption that just because a certain behavior or action has had the same result among everyone else who has tried it, "It's not going to happen to me." Addiction is a good example. "Those people who use heroin will get addicted, but that will never happen to me."

If we combine these two factors, along with what is often a dangerous misunderstanding of the concept of death, the risk of "accidentally" dying by suicide increases considerably. By exploring with a person their level of understanding of the possible consequence of a suicide attempt, we can sometimes use that information to prevent the attempt from happening.

For a person who sees suicide as a way to inflict guilt or exact revenge, I sometimes explain that when you are dead, you will not know how the people you left behind feel because you won't be around to see for yourself. I sometimes describe it as not having a skybox to sit in and look down at what others are feeling and doing in response to your suicide.

A client will often respond to this by saying, "I don't want to die. I just want to get back at my parents." This is when you can intervene and steer the person away from their suicidal ideation, directing them toward healthy ways of dealing with anger and complex feelings.

» WHAT HELPS?

I always believe we must gather information about the positives in a person's life. I want to know from a functional perspective what, if anything, helps my client feel better. I stress the term *functional* here because there are any number of dysfunctional ways clients try to cope with their feelings of depression and suicide.

For example, someone who tells me they drink or use marijuana on a regular basis to help themselves feel better is not necessarily a strategy I want to reinforce. This can be tricky because if those and similar behaviors (from the client's perspective) help them cope, it creates a dilemma for me. While marijuana is now legal in many states, is it the best coping mechanism?

Do I take those coping strategies away from the client by explaining their dysfunctional nature? What if a client thinks those strategies seem to be helping? Do I take the position of whatever works for them works for me?

This is difficult to answer, and everyone must decide how to approach this issue for themselves. I do not encourage or condone such behavior, nor do I criticize a client for their choices. Within certain limits, I do leave these decisions to them.

There's a basic tenet that says that when something is taken away from a client, it must be replaced with something else. So, if I can convince a client that drinking is not the best way to cope with depression, it becomes my responsibility to help them figure out other ways to cope.

In most cases, clients report more functional and healthy sources of support and encouragement from family, friends, clergy, etc. There are also healthy behaviors clients often report that range from exercising to reading, meditation, and prayer.

In this context, we must revisit the role of religion and religious beliefs as they relate to the issue of suicide. Unless you are a minister or pastoral counselor or in some other role defined by a faith-based approach, ethical standards dictate that you do not impose your religious beliefs on your clients in any circumstance.

As I mentioned earlier, arguing against suicide based on religious beliefs is hardly ever an effective approach. A client's religious beliefs are not to be challenged. This is a sure way to lose them.

This is where it gets tricky. Pastoral counselors and clergy will tell you that clients who come to them for help around their suicidal feelings are looking for assistance and direction not only from an emotional standpoint but from a religious one.

For clients with strong religious beliefs, the religious indictment of suicide can be an effective intervention tool. There is a difference, however, between a client who holds those beliefs and one who has those religious beliefs imposed upon them. Navigating those differences is important, especially when it comes to reinforcing functional, healthy coping mechanisms.

All this said, it is, of course, important to try to dissuade your clients from employing dysfunctional ways of coping. The trick here is to do so in a way that is not challenging or judgmental.

"How's that working for you?"

This question encompasses the approach you might take with clients in helping them to explore more functional ways of dealing with their feelings and depression. Of course, there is always the case of a client who says that their regular, heavy use of alcohol gets them through the day just fine. Arguing the point won't work. Suggesting more healthy alternatives might.

» **WHAT MAKES IT WORSE?**

Suicidal thoughts and feelings are fluid and occur on a continuum. There are times when the feelings, on a scale of one to ten, may be only a two or three, while at other times it could be eight, nine, or even ten.

Similar to how we explore what helps minimize a client's suicidal feelings, it is also important to understand what factors contribute to increasing those feelings. Some clients will be able to identify specific contributors, such as lack of sleep, stress at home or at work, conflicts in a relationship, and even something as seemingly simple as the time of day or day of the week.

As I described in discussing risk factors, Sunday evenings have been shown to be a particularly difficult time for people trying to cope with depression and suicide. Clients who live alone have often reported that Sunday evenings often intensify their feelings of loneliness and desperation. Others, even clients who do not live alone, say that the prospect of facing another Monday with no apparent improvement in their mood is just too much for them to face.

Whatever the factors may be that seem to increase your client's feelings of depression and suicide, they need to be identified and addressed. Try to be as specific as you can.

Many times, a client cannot identify specific contributors. You will have to help discover the possible whys of what makes them feel worse.

Take them through their daily routine, talk about the people in their life, and explore those relationships that might be causing them stress or create negative feelings. Diet, sleep, drug or alcohol use, behaviors of a more sedentary nature, and other concrete factors should also be explored.

There is another process-related dynamic that can significantly contribute to a person's suicidal feelings. Simply put, it's trying and failing.

In exploring with a client what they may have tried to do to help themselves feel better, they will often report a list of things they have tried and that none of them have worked.

"Nothing I do seems to be helping."

This is a response that I have heard many times from clients.

We need to find out what they have tried to do to help themselves and what strategies have worked to help them feel better. It is even more important to find out what has *not* worked.

These "failings" are crucial to understand for two reasons. First, you don't want to reinvent the wheel by suggesting a coping mechanism or strategy that the client may have tried with little success. Second, I want to know what they have tried, but more significantly, I want to know how they feel about the fact that these behaviors or strategies have not worked.

Clients will usually seek help only after they have tried everything they can without success. When I explore how they feel about this, they often report that they could not figure out a way to help themselves feel better, and they are now even more depressed about the fact that they failed. Discouragement can be a significant contributor to feelings of helplessness and hopelessness.

Reframing and positive reaffirmation are two techniques typically identified with family therapy, but they can also be useful in this context. Reframing means presenting something back to a client in a different way and from a perspective they may not have considered. Positive reaffirmation means taking something that could be interpreted as negative or dysfunctional and putting a positive spin on it.

A variation on these techniques can be used in situations such as the one described above. Here are a few examples of these techniques and how they might help your clients look at things from a different perspective.

"Well, it's good that you have eliminated all the things you know that haven't helped. You've saved us both a lot of work. Now, let's work together to see if we can identify some other approaches that might help."

"It sounds like you have been working really hard to try to fix things for yourself. I know how difficult that can be."

"You have a lot of strengths, but even the strongest of us can't always solve our problems on our own."

» **IS THERE ANYTHING THAT COULD MAKE IT BETTER FOR YOU?**

This question is similar to the previous question, but it deals more with a client's thought processes and other factors that might have a positive impact on their mood, self-image, and how they generally feel. It also looks at factors in their life that help them to have a more positive outlook and to feel more optimistic.

Asking about what could make it better also tries to address what I refer to as the client's list of *ifs* and *if onlys*. Think of this as a client's wish list in the context of cause and effect, i.e., "If this, then that," or "If only this, then that."

For example, a client may say, "If only I can get through the next few days, then I know I will start to feel better," or "If I could just find a job, then I can address some of my financial needs. That will help me feel less stressed."

While these two examples are somewhat realistic because they reflect a degree of reason and attainability, there are specific things that would need to happen for these two goals to be met. Getting through the next few days may require more intensive crisis therapy with the client. It might also require additional assistance by the client's support system.

Finding a job may be a goal that would have positive benefits, but it is probably more difficult to achieve. There are many variables that could affect one's ability to find employment. While this can be interpreted as a healthy goal, it would be important for the client and their therapist to process this in relation to how the client would feel if they do not find a job.

There is a secondary gain to be had while going through the job application process, and perhaps even landing an interview or two will give the client something to focus on and may contribute to a modicum of hope for their future. Landing a job is important to the client, but the therapist can point out that even if they are not successful, they did at least try. This is another example of the process being as important as the content.

On the other hand, let's look at the unrealistic "if onlys," things a client may think will help them feel better, which probably would if they happened, but more than likely, they never will: "If I could just win the lottery," or "If my boss would just stop yelling at me," or "If that teacher or my parents would just get off my back."

Winning the lottery can solve a lot of problems, but the last time I looked, the odds of winning anything significant were pretty slim. Controlling the behavior of others is just as improbable.

So, what happens when a client presents an unrealistic list of things they would like to see happen, which are, in fact, beyond their control? Here again, it is important to not discount the client or make them feel as if they are being totally unreasonable.

A more effective approach is to acknowledge that these wishes appear important to the client. The follow-up would be to look at each one from the standpoint of what would happen and to ask the right question, such as, "What will you do if you don't win the lottery? How will that make you feel?"

Then, it becomes a matter of exploring whether there are alternatives that would help the client feel better.

"Let's assume you don't win the lottery. What else could help you feel better?"

When a client's strategy for feeling better involves another person, especially when it means trying to control their behavior, it is important to help the client understand that even under the best of circumstances, none of us can control another person. Help the client understand that the issue is more about how they react to others, how it makes them feel, and explore how they can modify their own reactions and feelings about that other person.

Modifying the client's reactions includes exploring the client's vulnerabilities and what is often a perceived threat to their self-esteem and how others trigger those feelings. First, what does the other person say or do that prompts these feelings? Second, what can the client do to recognize these feelings, and how can you help them learn new ways of coping with them?

Keeping in mind that all things are relative, any criticism or negative feedback that we see as insignificant may be devastating to your client. It is important to understand how the dynamics and associated feelings of a suicidal individual may affect their response to such things. Low self-esteem and feelings of worthlessness are large contributing factors when it comes to understanding the importance that someone who is already in a vulnerable state may put on the opinion of others.

From my own experience, whenever I do a workshop, I always ask to see copies of the participants' evaluations. I pour through them and take heart from the largely affirmative ratings and comments that people make.

Invariably, there is always one or a small handful of evaluations that are less than complimentary. Despite an overabundance of positive reactions to my presentation, I may let a few negative ones bother me more than they probably should.

On a constructive note, I am always looking for ways to improve. Someone once said that our failures make us better. In my case, however, I would often let those few negative comments tap into something that reinforces a lingering feeling of inadequacy.

My reaction to those negative comments would drive my boss up the wall. He'd get frustrated with me, pointing out that I was pulling one bad review out of 100 good ones and letting it bother me.

It's taken me a long time to come to grips with the fact that I do that. Do I become suicidal as a result? No, but the dynamic is similar to the suicidal person's reaction to any negative feedback. I'm still working on it.

It can be difficult to get a depressed and/or suicidal client to understand how they can control their own feelings about how others treat them when so much of their own self-image is tied to the opinion of others. To a certain extent, it's basic to human nature, but we must all realize that depending on the opinion of others is not the only path to developing self-esteem.

I often hear myself reminding a client that they are important and have value. I do this when a client tells me that the only thing that will make them feel better depends on the behavior and attitude of others. My obvious response in this circumstance is meant to lead the client toward something they can do to help themselves feel better. The second piece of that is what we can do together to boost positive feelings.

Realistic expectations of themselves and others are important to examine with a client, but it's more crucial to help them realize that their reaction to the behavior of others is what's critical and that it can be controlled.

» **WHAT WOULD PUSH YOU OVER THE EDGE?**

Be careful with this one. This is not a question I routinely use, but it helps in cases when I feel like I am not getting enough information to do an adequate risk assessment.

It makes perfect sense when I see a client exhibit an understandable lack of trust toward me and they hesitate to disclose personal and painful information. This is especially true when we are meeting for the first time.

Another dynamic that often occurs is what I interpret to be another function of the client's depression. Maybe they are unable to organize themselves enough to communicate what they are thinking and feeling in a way that helps me understand their level of risk. In asking the question or trying to elicit information from a client about their risk, it is not unusual for them to simply say, "I just don't know."

Ironically, I do find most clients are readily able to identify and tell me what conditions in their life or what circumstances could occur that would make them feel worse. You must be careful with this because, here, again, you do not want to give a client the impression that their choice to go ahead and commit suicide is dependent on the behavior of someone else or external circumstances.

The intervention here is two-pronged. First, we aim to help the client understand that they are letting the thoughts, behavior, and opinions of others affect them in a way that is reinforcing thoughts of taking their own life. Second, we can help the client understand that while they have no control over the thoughts, behavior, and opinions of others, they *can* control how they choose to react.

The other consideration is the client's ability, or lack thereof, to manage their depression. A client will sometimes tell you that no matter what they do, they feel worse and worse. It becomes a matter of trying to determine where the line is that the client might cross that would put them at a higher level of risk.

There is another approach I use even less often, but I do if it seems necessary.

There are times, albeit rare, when a client cannot identify anything about themselves or their environment that has a positive or negative effect on them. There are also times when a client may use avoidance and not be forthcoming with information that would be helpful to me in completing an adequate risk assessment.

Here, again, we must understand that the cause of this behavior can be rooted in several places. It could be the client's mistrust of me or of people in general. It could be the client's discomfort with any suicidal thoughts or feelings they may be experiencing and their hesitancy to share those with anyone. It could also be a function of the client's depression, which could inhibit their ability to recognize and/or make sense of those thoughts and feelings.

Fear can be another reason for a client's unwillingness or inability to communicate their suicidal feelings. The basis for this fear is mostly twofold. One reason could be that they have tried to reveal their feelings to someone, only to have those feelings minimized or dismissed entirely. The fear could be that I might react the same way.

Another reason for not being open is that the client is, themselves, frightened by their own feelings. Suicidal ideation, especially in its most intense form, is scary. It can, and sometimes does, become all-encompassing to the point where any other thoughts or feelings, even those of a positive nature, are shut out.

The client not only fears for their own welfare; they also experience a fear that their ideation might engulf me as well. The last thing they want is to project their feelings onto someone else. There is also a fear that their ideation is so extreme that I, as the provider, will be unable to cope with their feelings and that I will abandon them in the same way that perhaps others have done.

In these circumstances, I have occasionally said something like this to a client: "Let's just be honest with each other, and you tell me in your own words how serious you are about wanting to kill yourself." In other words, let's just cut through everything and get down to the basics. It's sometimes helpful to have them gauge their feelings on a scale such as low, medium, or high.

This approach is somewhat aggressive and confrontational, which is why I do not recommend using it except under specific circumstances. You must assess and be somewhat predictive of how you think a client will react before committing to this approach.

You should also preface this question with something to the effect of "I understand this is a difficult conversation for you to have, and I understand that some of what I might be asking you is making you uncomfortable, but I am here to help you, so I just need to know certain things. I can assure you that whatever you tell me will not frighten me or scare me away."

Make it clear that whatever steps are taken in response to a client's reported level of risk will be done with as much input and cooperation by the client as possible.

Sometimes, clients are unable or unwilling to open up to you. Asking this question in a way that is supportive can convey a message to the client that you are here to help and that their suicidal ideation, no matter how intense, will not frighten you or chase you away.

» **WHAT CAN I DO FOR YOU?**

This is another question that is fraught with landmines. I suggest asking this in whatever form you choose so you can get your client to express what, if any, expectations they have of you. I've seen many clients respond to this question in a puzzled manner. They often say they don't know what I can do for them and then ask me to tell them what I can do.

On other occasions, clients have been specific about what they expect of me. Some of these expectations are reasonable and within the realm of what I can do for them in my role. Other times, their expectation is not possible for me to meet.

For example, a client might say, "I want you to call my boss and tell him to stop harassing me," or "I want you to tell my parents that I should be able to stay out until midnight."

Obviously, these are not things that fall within your responsibility, and here is how I usually respond to these kinds of requests: "No, that is not something I can or will do for you. But maybe we can figure out a way to help you address these issues with your boss, your parents, or whoever is causing you stress."

At that point, we might role-play. I might suggest that they write down their thoughts and feelings in the form of a letter, which may never actually be given to the person. Sometimes, I suggest that after writing the letter, the client rip it into pieces and throw it away.

In the case of parents, a spouse, or family members, I might suggest we invite that person to come in so that whatever concerns the client has can be addressed in the safety of a session.

Bottom line: Make sure you understand what the client expects of you.

9. ON THE FLIP SIDE

IMAGINE AN EXCHANGE like this and take a minute to consider your reaction.

Assessor: "Are you currently feeling suicidal?"
Client: "No!"
Assessor: "Thank God!"

While most clients are honest about their suicidal feelings and may be telling the truth, I need to hear more before I fully believe them. One clue is their reaction to the question.

Some people are puzzled. This is often a good indication that any thoughts of suicide were way beyond anything they had been considering.

Some get offended. "No, of course not. How could you even think that?" Again, a good indicator.

Some people are so depressed that the mere thought of taking any action, much less making a suicide attempt, is simply not within the realm of possibility.

While these may be relatively reliable indicators of a client's lack of any suicidal ideation, I need to know more to feel sure.

There's an old saying that fits this perfectly: "Don't believe everything you hear and only half of what you see." No surprise. Some clients are not totally honest when they say they don't feel suicidal.

This happens for a lot of reasons. It could be a lack of trust. It could be a function of depression that leads them to believe that no one, including you, would care how they feel. It could be feelings of shame about those feelings.

If someone tells you they are not having any suicidal feelings, your work is far from over. Do not, do not, *do not* take no at face value! You *must* conduct further explorations with the client to truly assess their current level of risk.

MORE QUESTIONS, HISTORY TIME

Whether your client is actively suicidal, reports any level of suicidal ideation, or has never considered suicide, you should gather additional information to complete your assessment. This is also a strategy that can be used to assess the validity of a person's denial of any ideation. History-taking is an effective tool.

If circumstances allow, this history can be helpful in your overall assessment of risk with any client, even those who report having any current ideation. The only exception might be if they are currently in the throes of a crisis that requires immediate attention. In those cases, history-taking probably needs to take a back seat.

There is also a need to assess a client's possible future risk. This is tricky and involves a certain amount of speculation on both your parts, but there are some relatively reliable predictive factors that can be considered.

Your client may feel uncomfortable with your additional probing. I tend to let them know that, while that may be the case, I ask these questions of everyone I see. It lends a sense of normalcy to the process.

» **HAVE YOU EVER FELT SUICIDAL?**

This question is helpful to assess a client's current level of risk for suicide. Previous suicidal feelings are an indicator of future risk.

» **IF YES, WHEN WAS THE LAST TIME?**

If the client reports having had suicidal feelings, you want to know how recently they experienced them. Someone who felt suicidal two days ago is at far greater risk than someone who says they felt suicidal a year ago and have had no recurrence of those feelings. Keep in mind that even someone who reports having not felt suicidal for the past year is still potentially at risk.

» **HAVE YOU EVER ATTEMPTED SUICIDE?**

This question is a crucial part of history-taking and should be explored whether the client reports having any ideation or not. It is important to know if your client has had any previous suicide attempts because this puts them at a higher risk for another attempt in the future. Even clients with no history of suicide attempts can still be at high risk. Like anything, this question is one part of a much bigger picture.

» **HOW RECENT WAS THE ATTEMPT?**

This is a simple question. The more recent, the more at risk.

» **WHAT METHOD WAS USED?**

I want to know what method a person used in their most recent suicide attempt. This will indicate the seriousness of the attempt and the level of potential lethality, based on the method used. Even a method that could be characterized as minimally lethal does not tell the whole story. Remember the woman who took four aspirin.

» **NOW WHAT?**

Much more information about previous attempts needs to be collected. In the next chapter, a section on postvention following a nonlethal attempt will cover this. The information we've covered here will help you assess current and future risk. The next issue is how to intervene at various stages of a suicide crisis, but before we do that, we must consider another foundational question.

PART FOUR

INTERVENTION

10. THE QUESTION

BEFORE WE DISCUSS interventions, a question begs consideration.

Does a person have the right to commit suicide?

Let's put it another way: Do *you believe* that people have the right to commit suicide if they choose to do so?

These are questions all of us need to ask ourselves and, more importantly, answer. As a professional practitioner, how you feel about a person's right to take their own life could impact how you approach this issue with a client.

No matter what you feel or believe about a person's right to die, can you leave those feelings and beliefs at the door? This question was a major principle in my graduate training. What do you bring to that situation, and how does it affect your work?

Societies around the world continue to struggle with questions of assisted suicide, death with dignity, a patient's right to be taken off life support, and the legality of suicide. While these are important issues, they are most often addressed through regulation and legislation.

Like anything else, however, we cannot legislate personal attitudes. When you are sitting face-to-face with a client who is contemplating suicide or someone who has just made a serious attempt, it is important to understand and appreciate how your personal feelings about a person's right to die may come into play.

Here are two examples.

An eighty-three-year-old man with no friends or family is living on Social Security in a small, subsidized apartment. He rarely goes out, except to buy groceries, which usually consist of canned stew, eggs, and a loaf of bread. Some mornings, his chronic arthritis makes it almost impossible to get out of bed. Most nights, he goes to sleep hoping he won't wake up.

A seventeen-year-old young woman, the oldest child in an intact upper middle-class family, is in her senior year in an advanced program at a well-funded suburban high school. She is active in student government and is a starter on the school volleyball team. Her boyfriend of two years, who is a year older and attending college away from home, has informed her, via email, that he has met someone else and has decided to break up with her. She feels as though her world has come to an end and isn't sure she can go on living anymore without her boyfriend.

Are either of these person's suicidal feelings more understandable than the other?

Does one person's circumstance make the prospect of suicide more understandable and potentially more "acceptable" to you than another's?

How do you feel about these two people, and how, if at all, will your feelings influence your approach with each of them?

In a perfect world, feelings would not influence you, but in the real world, they might. We cannot, and should not, make a value judgment about these people in either scenario. Your approach may, of course, be different based on circumstance. The important factor is to understand your role, in whatever capacity that may be, and fulfill the responsibilities regardless of the situation.

I highly recommend that you come up with answers to these basic questions and that you work through your feelings by yourself, through supervision or by some other means. I'm not suggesting that you compromise your beliefs, but when you work with a client, you must leave your own "stuff" at the door. One person's "right" may be another person's "wrong," but your job is to remain objective and focus on helping your client.

INTERVENTION STRATEGIES

There are basically three levels of intervention. The first is meant to prevent a suicide attempt from occurring. The second is an intervention when an attempt has been made. The third is called postvention, which follows a nonlethal attempt.

Before we discuss interventions, some concepts need to be understood.

HOW AND WHY SUICIDE PREVENTION WORKS

One requirement of my graduate program was to write a master's thesis. I did this as a group project with three classmates. We decided, based on research and an extensive review of the most current literature at the time (1980) regarding best practice models, to design a model suicide prevention program. We gathered information on existing programs and spoke to several people experienced with this topic.

Now, master's level social work students are not the greatest researchers. Yes, we took courses, and we learned about validity, reliability, and statistical significance, but we were not prepared to publish or even present scientifically based research and findings.

An old saying goes something like "a camel is nothing more than a horse designed by a committee." The four of us worked as a committee, but we each had our own opinions and ideas about what the final product should look like. When we finished our literature review, or so we thought, we felt we were ready to discuss our next step, which was to develop a program design.

Our faculty advisor was the professor who taught the research courses. She agreed that we had done a good job researching suicide prevention programs but that we had not yet made a convincing argument as to why suicide prevention programs should exist in the first place.

"Of course, suicide prevention programs are important," I said.

"Why?" she said. "Why are they important?"

"Because they save lives," I said. "They help prevent people from committing suicide."

As the discussion went on, our advisor continued to challenge us.

"If suicide prevention is effective, what makes it so? Specific techniques and approaches aside, is there a theoretical and clinical basis that can explain how and why suicide prevention works? What are the internal dynamics and feelings a person experiences when they are in the throes of a suicidal crisis? How do those dynamics and feelings affect effective intervention?"

Answering these questions forced us to discover and explain the justification for the mere existence of suicide prevention as a field of practice. More importantly for me, it provided the basis for how I developed my own approach to suicide prevention. What we learned became the driving force behind my beliefs and commitment to the notion that suicide can be prevented.

Suicide prevention does not work all the time. If it did, no one who ever called or came into a suicide prevention center or crisis intervention center would ever make an attempt.

We have seen cases of communities where suicide prevention centers opened, and the subsequent rate of suicide went up. There are many theories as to why this occurs, the most accepted being that the higher rate was due to improved and more accurate reporting.

When suicide prevention works, based on our research and my own experience, it does so for two reasons. First, suicidal thoughts and feelings are temporary.

A myth says that once a person is suicidal, they are always suicidal. That is simply not true. A person may feel suicidal today and not tomorrow. They may be suicidal next week but not have suicidal thoughts or feelings for the next six months. In our master's thesis, we came up with a phrase to describe this phenomenon: "the transitory nature of the suicidal ideation."

Suicidal feelings are just that. They are feelings, and like any others, one cannot hold onto them indefinitely. The same is true regarding the intensity of those feelings. Someone may be experiencing strong feelings of wanting to kill themselves for a few hours or days, but those feelings, like most human emotions, will eventually subside. The feelings may reappear, but there will also be times when they are not present.

The second concept that explains why and how suicide prevention works is ambivalence. In this context, ambivalence refers to the wish to die and the desire to live going on at the same time. Those concomitant urges ebb and flow at varying levels and times.

Another myth says that people who commit suicide must have really wanted to die. Even for the seriously suicidal individual, the wish to die may be very high, and the wish to live may be very low, but they both exist.

These mixed feelings about wanting to live or die are why someone will overdose and then call a family member, friend, or suicide prevention center. In one case, a gentleman called a local community hotline on the premise that he just wanted to tell someone he was going to kill himself. He did not want any help or someone to intervene, and under no circumstances was anyone to call his sister, whose address and phone number were available.

Both of these concepts were clearly evident in the case of Don, as described in the prologue, although I did not know enough at the time to put a label on them. They are also the driving force behind the title of this book.

11. THREE LEVELS OF INTERVENTION

JUST AS WE live in the past, present, and future, when it comes to suicide, we will inevitably face intervention challenges before, during, or after an attempt.

BEFORE AN ATTEMPT

Many times, we are confronted with someone who is *actively suicidal*. While they may have not yet made an attempt, the level of risk is certainly high.

We discussed the components of a risk assessment in previous chapters, which is a crucial factor in this scenario. Intervening to prevent an actual attempt is an entirely different matter.

The concept of the temporary nature of one's suicidal ideation is important to understand because of its implication as to how I would choose to intervene.

For example, I will never say, "Don't kill yourself." I will say, "Don't do it now." I will suggest that they put it off for an hour or two, a day or two, or however much time you can get the person to agree to.

In the meantime, I would say, "Let's talk about how and why you got to this point and what we can do to address the situation." I would acknowledge the fact that after we've had a chance to talk, if they still want to kill themselves, they could certainly do that.

Of course, this oversimplifies the process I go through. You will get varying levels of resistance to this approach. It is important not to argue with the client; instead, offer alternatives.

We talked earlier about tunnel vision and how difficult it is for someone feeling suicidal to see any other solution to their problems. The same is true with a person's suicidal ideation. Often, they get so locked into the fact that they have decided to kill themselves that it does not occur to them that they have choices.

Most often, the notion that they can change their mind regarding their decision to commit suicide does not even enter the realm of possibility for them.

"I don't understand," said a forty-two-year-old woman sitting across from me. "I don't understand what you're telling me."

"I'm trying to say that you can change your mind about killing yourself. You can put it off for as long as you like, or you can decide not to do it at all."

She was clearly skeptical.

"Why would I do that? You know it's hard enough for me to make decisions about anything these days."

"Yes, depression has a way of doing that. It slows everything down, including our thought processes. It can make you almost immobile."

"It sure does in my case. Some mornings, I can't even get out of bed or decide what clothes to put on!"

"I get it, but you made the decision to kill yourself, didn't you?"

She managed a grin. "I did, didn't I? So, why would I change my mind now?"

"Because, like anything, you can. Listen, it's up to you. All I'm suggesting is that you put it off for a while, that's all."

The strategy of suggesting that a person delay their suicide attempt, rather than arguing with them against making the attempt at all, serves several explicit and implicit purposes. First, it tells the person that I am not taking an adversarial position. The basic rule of psychotherapy that directs us to start where the client is and go with them also holds true here.

This approach also avoids getting into a power struggle over who has control of the situation. In many cases, an actively suicidal individual feels like they have lost control of everything in their life. Killing themselves is sometimes looked at as the only way they have to take back control, so the last thing you want to do is take that feeling away from them.

However, you can help a client understand that, while committing suicide may be the ultimate act of control, they also have control over when they choose to kill themselves. Sometimes, a client may be open to the idea that they also can put off the attempt until later, if they so choose.

Another approach is to work with the client to understand and accept the notion that they can take control by deciding not to commit suicide. Oftentimes, a person is just not at that point yet, so you should be careful in using this as a strategy. Remember tunnel vision.

The other more implicit aspect of this approach is that you are simply trying to buy time. Over time, suicidal feelings will generally subside, and your goal is to get to the point where their suicidal feelings start to diminish.

When this is done well, a person's suicidal ideation will lessen, partially because of your conversation with them regarding the issues that brought them to this point. Also, by getting them to discuss their problems, you can hopefully help them to feel less hopeless.

There is as much value in what you say and do as there is in the process of getting a person to open up to you. There is also value in focusing the conversation away from a client's suicidal ideation and onto other aspects of their current circumstance.

Bottom line: the more time you can buy, the better chance you have of a client feeling less suicidal.

Another myth worth mentioning is that someone who commits suicide must have really wanted to die. The concept of ambivalence would seem to challenge this line of thinking. Even someone who died by suicide had more than likely experienced a certain level of ambivalence. In those cases, the desire to die would have far outweighed the wish to live. Sadly, in those cases, we will never know for sure.

Another common myth is that people who talk about suicide don't really mean it. The reality? People talk about suicide because they are feeling suicidal. They also talk about it because, consciously or not, they most likely do want someone to intervene.

Even in circumstances where there is a much stronger wish to live, a suicidal individual will often create roadblocks and make it difficult for anyone to help. I do not view this as an unwillingness to accept help. I interpret this kind of push-pull behavior as a function of depression, a result of feeling hopeless and helpless, and a greatly diminished sense of self-esteem that basically says, "I'm not worth helping."

Resistance comes in many forms and can often get in the way of effective interventions. It is important to understand the dynamics behind someone's resistance and to address its behavioral manifestations and source. Hopefully, this can ease the resistance so you can begin to address your client's problems and concerns.

Addressing a suicidal individual's ambivalent feelings is the second point of intervention. This must be done cautiously. For example, I would never confront a client with the idea that they don't really want to die. That would only result in an argument as to why they want to kill themselves.

I take a slightly different approach by steering the conversation in a more positive context. I will ask the person to tell me about the part of them that wants to live. Framing the question this way can prompt various responses.

Hopefully, a person will admit that a part of them wants to live but that feelings of hopelessness and wanting to die are so overwhelming that they just don't see a way out. This is when you can begin to explore alternatives and eventually help them see that there are other less destructive ways of dealing with their problems.

The conversation with my client continued.

"You know, there's something else we can talk about."

"And what would that be?" she asked.

"Well, it has to do with the fact that you're here and we're talking."

She became somewhat impatient with me. "So, what's that got to do with anything? We talk all the time. We talk about me. We talk about my rotten husband. We talk about how much I hate my job. We talk about a lot of things."

"Yes, we do, but today we're talking about how you want to kill yourself. You've never brought that up before. So, I must ask, why now?"

"Things seem to be getting more and more out of hand. I feel like I can't deal with life anymore." She sounded almost desperate. I leaned forward and looked straight at her.

"So, suicide feels like a possible answer. But I still must ask. Why tell me? Why come in today and tell me? Why not just stay home and go through with it?"

She shrugged. "I don't know. I hadn't thought about it. I just thought, well, today's my appointment, so I should come in."

"That's one reason, but I think there's something else going on. I need you to explore something with me."

"Okay, what would that be?"

"Tell me about another part of you. Tell me about the part of you that wants to live."

It was as if I had turned a switch. Tears came, and then she started crying, sobbing. She grabbed the ever-present box of tissues from the side table.

"How do you know? How do you know about that?" she asked between her sobs.

"I'm smart," I said.

I was trying to lighten the mood. Maybe not the best answer, but I knew this client well, and we often used humor in our discussions.

"Not really," I went on. "I just know that there's a part of you that feels that way."

"It's true," she answered. "You're right. It's there. I feel it, but I just can't get past how awful I feel to let it in. Is that so terrible?"

"Not at all, but it's that part we can work on."

We explored her ambivalence regarding her suicidal feelings. She was finally able to admit that killing herself would not be the answer.

Even though the problems that brought her to this point were still there, she admitted that killing herself would not solve anything. In the following sessions, we managed to make some progress, but we still had a long way to go.

Not all examples of ambivalence are so obvious, and the fact that I already had a therapeutic relationship with this client made a difference in my approach.

The more difficult situation involves a person who responds by saying there is no part of them at all that wants to go on living. Here again, it is important not to argue or try to convince them otherwise.

My approach is to address the process. How long have you felt this way? What brought you to this point? Was there a time when you felt you might be able to go on living? What was going on at that time? Other areas will need to be explored, but this approach will provide a baseline for where you want to go.

To reiterate, when suicide prevention works, it's because of these two basic reasons. However, in some circumstances, addressing the temporary nature of suicidal feelings and a person's ambivalence about wanting to die will simply not be effective. That's when you may need to take a more active role in preventing the person from committing suicide.

For a person who is actively suicidal and unwilling or unable to agree to not harm themselves, you can take steps to ensure their safety. This could mean involving family, friends, or other sources of support. It could also mean taking steps to have the client evaluated for possible involuntary hospitalization or admission to a twenty-four-hour crisis center.

These are not easy decisions to make, but they are sometimes necessary. I believe that if you are going to err, do so on the side of caution. Some clinicians worry about the repercussions of taking such actions and that the client might be angry with them or terminate services. Those are valid concerns, but it is important to appreciate the fact that, while the client may be angry with you, they are still alive.

DURING AN ATTEMPT

The scenario is not uncommon: Someone cuts their wrists or takes an overdose of medication and then calls 911 or a local crisis line to report what they have just done. They don't want help. They just want someone to know what they did before they die. Yeah, right!

The reason someone makes that kind of call is because, at some level, they *do* want someone to intervene. Otherwise, why make the call in the first place? Again, remember Don. This brings us back to the concept of ambivalence.

I have heard of many cases of callers to a local crisis line who report what they have done and insist that they do not want any help. It's the ambivalence that motivates people to do such things. In these cases, we must listen to what the person is saying, but also to what they are "not" saying. Put another way, the mere fact that they called is enough of an indicator that they *do* want someone to intervene.

When confronted with a suicidal crisis, some basic things will help you and your client.

Breathe!

Especially if you are less experienced, when you get that proverbial "I've got a gun in my hand" call, you will gasp. Take a moment, take the phone away from your mouth, take a deep breath, let it out slowly, and then jump back in.

Don't rush.

Most of the time, you will have time to intervene. Barring a gunshot or someone bleeding arterially, you have time to gain the caller's trust and have them help you help them. Pushing too hard or moving too fast may put a caller off, and you may lose them.

"Put the gun down."

Yes, literally. If the caller is holding a gun or knife, ask them to put it down. If they refuse, don't argue. Come back to it later.

"I know you're still sitting there with that gun in your hand. Could you put it down now?"

Even better if you can get them to put it in a drawer, somewhere out of sight, or—even better—in another room.

Don't take away their "right" to pick the gun back up. "Please, put the gun down. If you want to pick it back up, that's okay, but could you just put it down while we're talking?"

Still refusing? Try this: "You know, I'm really nervous about you holding that gun, and I'm afraid something might happen while we're talking. I'd feel a whole lot better if you'd put it down." You'll be amazed at what people will do for someone else to feel better. It doesn't work every time, but it's worth a try.

If the caller is armed and you involve police or EMTs, make sure you inform the caller that you have done so. This is debatable, and I have had many discussions about this, but I don't want to keep any secrets from the caller. Trust is key.

You should also inform any responders that the client is armed, if that is the case. Their safety is an important factor.

Even though a caller might not say it, they *do* want help. Some will tell you they do not want you to do anything, but I always assume that since they picked up a phone and called, they want me to do something.

Stay away from clichés, such as "I'm glad you called today." Most of the time, the caller couldn't care less about how *you* feel. That's not why they're calling.

Don't confront a caller's ambivalence too early. You know why they called. They don't always know, except that something prompted them to reach out. Avoid statements like "I know you don't really want to die." The fact is, if they've already taken any pills, at some level, they probably do want to die. Ambivalence swings both ways.

As best and as soon as you can, assess the caller's physical condition. Are they bleeding? Are they nodding off? You may have to ask, so explain that you need to know so you can help them.

Have a team available, or at least one other person to assist you. If this is not possible, you should be able to contact someone on another phone, be it EMTs or a supervisor.

You may be in a situation where you must put the caller on hold to make another call. Obviously, this is not ideal, but if you must, make sure the caller understands that you will get right back to them as quickly as possible.

Let's take a second here to remember an old line and give ourselves a chance to smile, even in the context of a dark discussion.

"You know you're having a bad day when you call the suicide hotline and get put on hold."

All joking aside, any caller will want to know why you are doing this. Don't lie. Explain that you need to reach out for assistance should the situation warrant it. Technology being what it is today, you probably have options in terms of how to deal with this.

Under no circumstances should you tell the caller where you are or if you are alone.

Unless the caller blocked their number, write it down right away. You can usually retrieve it from your phone's listing of recent calls or caller ID. If none of this works, ask the caller for the number they are calling from. Explain that you need it in case you are cut off. In some ways, this helps a caller feel more like you are there to help.

Ask if anyone is with them or somewhere nearby. I know of several situations, especially with adolescents, where the caller was in their room, having taken an overdose, and the parents were in the house. Nowadays, with cell phones, this is becoming more and more problematic.

Your agency, program, or practice should try to be proactive. Establish a positive working relationship with your local police, EMTs, hospital emergency department, etc. Meet with folks. If you work in a combined urban/rural area, you will want to include county sheriffs and state police officials.

Let these potential resources know who you are and what your service is about. I know one director of a crisis team who did a ride-along with the local police for a month, which did wonders for their relationship.

Learn your state laws and professional standards regarding the issues of duty to warn and protect.

Document, document, document. Put everything in writing, in whatever format your organization requires. Take notes as you go. There is no way you will remember everything later.

Understand that despite your best efforts, people will die by suicide. This is where the need for supervision and a good personal and professional support system can be invaluable. Even the best of us will experience feelings of failure and a sense of "I could have, should have, would have done more." If a client's death, in any form, but especially by suicide, doesn't bother you on some level, maybe it's time to take up another line of work.

AFTER A NONLETHAL ATTEMPT

Few people will seek out follow-up services after a suicide attempt unless those services have been recommended by someone or a referral has been made. It's rare when someone comes in on their own accord because they realize they need help.

Survivors of a nonlethal suicide attempt often do not seek treatment. Their feeling is "I tried it, I did not die, I feel okay, and I'm just going to go home and get on with my life."

Families, particularly in cases involving a child or adolescent, can also contribute to the misdirected belief that once their child is relatively stable and medically cleared, the problem has been solved. I have seen parents in a hospital emergency room or crisis center refuse referrals for ongoing services, saying they will simply take their child home, and everything will be fine.

Another reason why survivors of nonlethal suicide attempts do not seek treatment is because they have become so discouraged and even more depressed that they tried to kill themselves and were not even able to do it. This thinking can intensify feelings of hopelessness and helplessness. These feelings can become so pervasive that the person believes they are even more beyond hope and help. Clearly, this individual is at a very high risk for making another suicide attempt.

Another scenario occurs for some people who survive a suicide attempt and conclude, after their attempt, that they really did not want to die. Some will take their survival as a sign, even religious in nature, that perhaps their problems aren't that serious after all. This results in an apparent "lightening of the load." Some report the experience as being almost cathartic.

We often refer to it as "a rush to health." In some cases, this experience can trigger a positive change with lasting effects. In most situations, however, these positive feelings are short-lived, and the person eventually finds themselves back in the throes of their depression.

One could make the argument that no matter how brief, the person felt better. Why not leave them alone and let them embrace their newfound sense of well-being? While I usually support that approach, I also know that there will often be an eventual crash and burn.

It is important for someone in this situation to understand what is happening and to seek treatment services to help maintain the good feelings they are experiencing. I also want them to understand that there may be a point when their depression returns and that it is important for them to reach out for help when that happens. With that in mind, there are questions (yes, more questions) I want to pose to someone seeking help after a nonlethal suicide attempt.

WHAT MADE YOU DECIDE TO SEEK HELP?

Considering that many people do not seek treatment after a suicide attempt, we must gain a good understanding of why a client decides to come in. Just like any other situation, when a client or family seeks assistance, the motivation behind someone seeking treatment following a suicide attempt gives me a lot of information.

A client seeking services on their own because they realize they need help is the best-case scenario. However, this is probably not why most people seek help. Usually, someone who has survived a suicide attempt will seek services for other reasons:

1. They were referred by a hospital emergency department, crisis intervention service, or suicide hotline.
2. They were brought in, somewhat against their will, by a parent, spouse, friend, or other family member.
3. Even though they do not believe they have a problem, they agreed to come in for one session to have a professional validate their belief that they are fine and to convince others who may have accompanied them that they do not need any help.

I have had occasions with children and adolescents where the school would not allow the student to return to school following a suicide attempt until they were "cleared" and determined to no longer be at risk. This is not something I would ever agree to because I believe that in these circumstances, there is no such thing as no risk.

I also believe that there is an implicit message delivered by the school that the student is being punished for their behavior. I would never want to reinforce this. I would, with appropriate releases, pass my professional opinion on to the school, but then it is their place to decide.

Addressing a client's motivation for treatment is not much different than addressing the motivation of anyone who comes in to see you. However, there is one major difference: the behavior that brought the person in to see you could have resulted in their death. That is different from a child who is brought in because of ADHD symptoms or an adult with an anxiety disorder. Sometimes it is a matter of life or death.

Many people try to downplay the situation, and I have had clients say that it was no big deal, that they don't understand why everyone seems so upset by what happened. Low self-esteem and self-image contribute to a client's perception and puzzlement as to why others reacted so strongly to their attempt.

One way to address these issues is to help them understand that, while they may not feel good about themselves, other people value them and are worried. Convincing someone that others really care is often met with skepticism and disbelief. Occasionally, I will try an approach, such as "The big deal is, you almost died."

You will hear a variety of reactions to this statement. One client who was referred to me responded with "So what!" Others have been surprised and tell me it never occurred to them that this might happen. Others report being frightened.

When I refer to the possibility that they could have died, it often becomes a wake-up call. That said, some are angry about not dying. Some feel guilty, while others tell me it helped them realize how serious their problems are.

The "so what" response, whether intentional or not, is always provocative. The unconscious (or conscious) meaning behind this response says a lot about how this client feels about themselves and their relationships. I suggest exploring what they meant by their response.

I once had a middle-aged man referred to me after being treated for cutting his wrists. His wife discovered him on the floor of their bathroom. The bandages were clearly visible. He did not try to hide them.

"You say 'so what.' Does that bother you?" I asked.

"No, not really," he responded emphatically.

"Why not?" I asked.

Note: I was taught to never ask "Why?" because all you get back is a rationalization, but I figured after forty-some years in the field, I can ask what I want. We social workers are notorious for asking questions.

"Because maybe I would be better off if I were dead," he said.

"Better off in what way?" I wanted to explore any issues related to self-esteem that might be contributing to his ideation.

"I would not have to worry about anything. All my problems would go away, and no one else would have to worry about me anymore."

"What is so bad about people worrying about you?"

"It's not fair to them. They have better things to do than worry about me."

"So," I posed. "You think they would be better off without you? Has anyone ever said that to you?"

He smirked. "Well, not in so many words."

"Then, how do you know it's true?" I asked.

"I know because that's how I would feel," he explained.

I needed him to clarify.

"Okay, so let me understand," I started. "If someone in your family was depressed for a long time and eventually committed suicide, that would be okay with you because it would relieve you of the burden of having to worry about them. Is that right?"

"Well, not exactly. I guess I would feel bad about what they did and that they were gone."

"Would you miss them?"

"Of course," he said.

I knew where I was going with this line of questioning. "Would you wonder if there was something you could have done to stop them from killing themselves?"

He paused and then answered, "Probably. I guess so."

"Do you think they would be worth saving?"

He looked almost surprised by the question. "Well, yeah. Who wouldn't think that?"

"So, how is that any different for you? How is it that you don't believe you would be worth saving? How is it that you believe that everyone would be better off without you?"

My goal was to challenge, in a supportive way, the client's self-image, their sense of worth to themselves and others, and their assumptions about what others think. It took some time, but this client finally admitted that there were people who probably did care about him. We discussed how his depression interfered with him accepting this fact. It was the opening that I was hoping for.

We all make assumptions, and clients do the same about themselves and the world around them. My family therapy professor referred to this as the assumptive system, a system of beliefs based on what are usually untested theories and hypotheses. The goal is to help a client realize that their assumptions may not be realistic.

Sometimes, our job is to simply help a client see things differently. This may seem simple, but it is by no means easy.

QUESTIONS REGARDING A PREVIOUS ATTEMPT

At some point during the initial interview following a nonlethal suicide attempt, I want to get specific information from a client, as previously discussed. However, if their attempt is recent, you should ask these questions more cautiously and monitor their reaction.

A client's wounds, figuratively and sometimes literally, are still fresh. Unless this is a returning client, this is probably your first encounter, and they might understandably present as being guarded.

On a practical level, it would be helpful to get a copy of the patient's report from the emergency room, crisis service, or any program or service they might have utilized prior to seeing you. Of course, none of this information is available unless the client, parent, or guardian signs a release of information.

Under ideal circumstances, the crisis service would have had the client sign a release so they could make the referral to you and share information. How quickly that information gets to you will vary, and you may not have the luxury of waiting. This puts the burden on you to gather as much information from the client as possible.

In the case of a minor, you can discuss the situation with a parent or guardian, but not surprisingly, they may not have all the facts. All things being equal, the client is usually your best and most accessible source. Your clinical judgment must guide you about how hard and far you push them to get what you need.

Despite any roadblocks, you can and should explore other issues with a client.

» **WHAT WAS YOUR INTENTION?**
» **WERE YOU TRYING TO DIE?**

Understanding a person's motives will impact your approach to treatment. A person who reports a serious intention of wanting to die will require a different type of intervention than someone who attempted suicide because of desperation and an inability to find a solution to their problems.

While these motives may sound alike, they are not. One concrete difference is whether the client has come to see you voluntarily. Resistance to assistance comes in many forms. A client who says, "Just leave me alone. I just want to die" is a much higher risk than someone seeking treatment because they hope to find a solution to their problems and an alternative to suicide.

» **WHAT HAPPENED?**
» **WHY DID YOU NOT DIE?**

These questions give you the opportunity to understand the circumstances of your client's suicide attempt and why it did not result in their death. It also reveals if they built in a rescue scenario.

I categorize someone's rescue as being active or passive. An active rescue means the suicide attempter actively reached out and involved someone else in the prevention of their death. For example, someone who takes an overdose and then notifies a family member, friend, or emergency hotline is actively seeking to be rescued. This is a common situation.

The second category involves a circumstantial or unsolicited intervention that prevented the individual from dying. Perhaps a family member or friend discovered the person who took a lethal overdose and then intervened by calling EMTs or got them to an emergency department.

Sometimes, we see a person truly intent on dying, but something went "wrong." The gun misfired, a mixture of medication and alcohol was not high enough in dosage or caused the person to vomit the material, or a jump from a high place did not result in death.

Some people build in a rescue as part of their suicide plan. Maybe their intent was to not die but to use their attempt as a form of manipulation or for attention-getting purposes. Unfortunately, just as a plan of someone who intends to die by suicide does not always go the way they hoped, a plan that includes a rescue can also be affected by unforeseen circumstances.

One such case involved a teenage girl and her mother. The mom was a single parent and worked full-time to support herself and her daughter. Though this was not an ideal situation, Mom believed that her sixteen-year-old daughter would be safe at home for the couple hours between when she got home from school and Mom came home from work.

The daughter had a history of mild depression and some unresolved issues related to her parents' divorce. Mom was aware of these feelings, and she and her daughter were actively involved in family therapy at the agency where I served as program director.

There was no history of suicidal ideation and no reason to believe the girl was at high risk. However, she often expressed feelings of frustration and anger about her situation and the fact that neither of her parents seemed to understand how she was feeling.

Mom's work schedule was routine. She left work every day at 5 p.m. and, depending on traffic, would be home between 5:30 and 5:45 each night.

We can only speculate about why this girl attempted suicide. We learned later, based on medical reports and other information, that the lethal combination of alcohol and sleeping pills she ingested were probably taken after 5 p.m.

With that information and what we knew about this young girl and her history, we concluded with relative certainty that she did not intend to die as the result of the overdose. Knowing that her mother arrived home at relatively the same time every evening, it was safe to conclude that she had every intention of being found and saved.

In this case, unfortunately, an unforeseen variable interfered with the daughter's apparent rescue plan. As it turned out, Mom had to work late that evening and did not get home until after seven. By the time she returned home, it was too late.

Just like this tragedy, we see numerous cases of people who have died by "accident" as the result of a suicide attempt. With every intention of being found and saved, there are sometimes one or more variables that interfere with that plan. The result is devastating.

» **HOW DID YOU FEEL ABOUT NOT DYING?**

This question is meant to discover a person's motives behind their suicide attempt. It is also one of the more direct ways of assessing their future risk.

For example, someone who says, "I was really glad I survived because I realized that I did not want to die," or "It's okay because I was just doing it for attention anyway," is at a relatively low risk for future attempts. Again, I stress the word *relatively*.

The client who responds by saying, "I was mad as hell because I really wanted to die," is obviously at a high risk for another attempt.

» **DOES ANYONE ELSE KNOW ABOUT YOUR ATTEMPT?**

As difficult as it may be to believe, many people have attempted suicide and survived without anyone's knowledge or involvement. Sometimes, that is by design. Other times, it is because a person lives alone and makes an attempt that does not result in their death and does not require any medical attention or intervention.

Regardless of the situation, it is important to know who, if anyone, is aware that this person attempted suicide. This question also sets the stage for the next one.

» **WHAT WAS THEIR REACTION?**

Family members and friends usually become aware of a person's suicide attempt in one of two ways. First, they may have been directly involved, such as finding the person unconscious but alive after an overdose or somehow involved in the person's rescue.

The second way is for the person who made the attempt to tell family members or friends. We would hope, and assume, that parents, for example, would have firsthand knowledge of a suicide attempt by their child, but sadly, this is not always the case.

Will was a seventeen-year-old boy who came to me at his parents' request because he was having behavioral issues and unpredictable mood swings. I must give credit to these parents because they were insightful enough to understand their son's need for professional help.

As usual, I asked this young man about any suicidal thoughts and feelings he might be experiencing.

"I don't understand," the boy's mother said. "Why are you asking him about that?"

I tried to reassure her. "It's routine. I ask that question of everyone, even if it seems irrelevant. It's just a part of my regular assessment."

I turned my focus back to Will. He looked at me and then at his mother as he rolled up the sleeves of his shirt. A hastily rigged bandage was wrapped around each of his wrists. Will turned his hands to show his parents what he had done.

"I did this night before last," he said.

Will's mother started to cry. His father was wide-eyed with shock and surprise.

"We had no idea," his father said. "We knew he was having problems, but this? This? We had no idea things were this bad."

Will's mother found her voice and looked at Will. "Why? Why would you do this? What's so bad that would make you do this?"

I listened to his parents and then looked at Will.

"We'll get to the why in a while, but tell me, Will, what were you trying to do?"

His father interrupted before Will could answer. "What kind of question is that? Isn't it obvious what he did?"

"Not always," I tried to explain. "That's why I want to know. So, Will, why?"

Will stared at the floor. "I don't know. I just felt like, I don't know, like I was getting in the way."

"Getting in the way of what?" I asked.

"I don't know. Like I was getting in the way of everyone else. I mean, look at us. Look at where we are."

I tried to lower my head to meet his stare. "I'm not sure what you mean. Where are you?"

"Here!" he said loudly. "I mean, why are we even here? Everyone's in such a panic about me. They all worry about me too much."

I leaned even further forward. "So, you thought, what? I can guess, but you tell me. What was going through your head?"

"I thought, well, maybe, maybe if I wasn't here, they wouldn't have to worry no more."

"Oh, Will, oh, Will, we would never think like that," his mother said.

His father spoke up. "Listen, Son, no matter what, we are here for you. We never have, and never will, think of you that way. You hear me?"

We talked more, and I needed to get additional information about Will's attempt. The only thing he could find to use was a paint scraper, which, thankfully, did little serious damage. At my request, Will undid one of the bandages to show only surface scratches.

"I tried to go deeper," Will said. "But it hurt too much. Then, I got scared and just stopped. I guess, maybe I really didn't want to do it."

Surface scratches such as these are commonly referred to as hesitation marks, minor scratches that don't result in serious wounds. This is often the experience of someone whose wish to die is not the primary factor in their attempt. It also speaks volumes about their level of ambivalence.

Sometimes, such wounds are more related to the method that was used, as in this case. It's important to distinguish between the apparent level of ambivalence and the less than effective method of choice to assess the person's actual intent.

Referring back to Will and his parents, these were good people. It occurred to me that they were well-intentioned, but the fact that they knew nothing about their son's suicide attempt and that he chose not to tell them about it indicated some areas of concern that would need to be addressed.

Once Will's parents became aware of the situation, they reacted appropriately and cooperatively with treatment. They were motivated to improve their relationship with their son and do whatever they could to help him. This is the type of reaction that someone who is depressed and suicidal wants and needs, as it can, and often does, have a positive impact on the risk of any future attempts.

The reaction of others is a significant contributing factor when assessing someone for future risk, whether those responses follow an actual attempt or through one's communication of their suicidal thoughts or feelings. When people respond with care and a willingness to help, it may not be enough to prevent future attempts, but it is certainly a positive factor.

On the other hand, responses such as, "That's so stupid!" or "You shouldn't think that way" will certainly not help the situation.

A fourteen-year-old girl was brought into an emergency room from school after she was found having taken an overdose of pills. The mother was contacted, and she came immediately. After the daughter was successfully treated, the mother was allowed to see her.

The mother glared at her daughter, and the first words out of her mouth were not good. "How dare you do this to me!" she exclaimed. "How dare you put your father and me through this!"

Obviously, this is not the reaction one would hope for in this circumstance. We cannot be sure that the mother's reaction would cause her daughter to try again, but it's safe to say that it would not have a positive effect in reducing her risk.

» **ANY OTHER PREVIOUS ATTEMPTS?**

If there have been previous attempts, I may not necessarily go through the entire list of questions we have discussed, but I would pursue basic information about the attempt(s).

- » **HOW LONG AGO DID THEY OCCUR?**
- » **WHAT METHOD WAS USED?**
- » **IF THERE HAS BEEN MORE THAN ONE ATTEMPT, HOW FAR APART WERE THEY?**
- » **WERE THEY DAYS APART, WEEKS, OR MONTHS?**

The relationship of previous attempts to a client's current situation is important, especially when it comes to understanding motivation and meaning of those attempts and their relevance to the client's current situation.

- » **DID YOU SEEK PROFESSIONAL HELP?**

All too often, people leave emergency rooms or crisis centers or finish telephone conversations with a local suicide prevention hotline and never seek follow-up care. When I worked at a large family service agency, we did a study and found that even though referrals were routinely made by the crisis center for follow-up services, only 50 percent of those persons kept their appointment, and only half of those returned after their first session.

We know there are flaws in the mental health system that contribute to this lack of follow-up care, even if it does not involve a suicide attempt. However, many of our clients believed that once their initial crisis was resolved, everything was fine, and they could get on with their lives without a need for ongoing services.

There is a certain legitimacy to this kind of thinking. Some mental health experts believe that dealing with crises as they occur, as opposed to burdening someone with the responsibility of participating in ongoing treatment, is an acceptable approach. Others believe follow-up care is necessary to address the ongoing issues. Regardless, it is important to find out what, if any, ongoing services the person might have received after their suicide attempt.

I also want to know if they feel that those services have been helpful. What worked, and what didn't? That helps clarify my approach and avoid areas where no progress has been made.

» HOW DO YOU FEEL NOW?

This question is meant to assess a client's current emotional state. Their response will also help to provide an indication of their current risk of making another attempt.

Some clients have difficulty verbalizing exactly how they feel. Three choices can make it easier for them to describe how they feel now.

Think of a client's responses as a continuum. Ask this question through a comparative lens. Better than? Worse than? The same as? Yesterday? A week ago? An hour ago? This gives the client the opportunity to compare their current mood and level of functioning to a previous point in time. It also provides you with lots of useful information.

A complicating factor around this is how a client was feeling physically before their attempted suicide. For example, are there lingering physical issues as a result of their attempt?

I know of a young man who jumped from a two-story building and survived, but he came away with a severe head injury and broken vertebrae. Despite several surgeries and a lengthy rehab, he was never quite himself again. Ironically, he reported that he no longer felt depressed or suicidal and that regardless of his injuries, he was glad he had not died.

So, are things better for this client after his attempt? In some ways, yes. In other ways, obviously not. Either way, the client's perspective is what counts.

Medical providers will heal physical wounds, set broken limbs, and help people learn to walk again. Our role is to help clients understand the emotional conditions that led them to make a suicide attempt in the first place and to help them find new and better ways of coping so that this behavior is not repeated.

» HOW CAN I HELP?

As previously mentioned, this question can open several doors for you to intervene. If the circumstances that led to a suicide attempt are external, such as a client's relationship with a significant other, being bullied, or losing a job, there is not much you can do to change those circumstances. What you can do is help a client understand how those situations affect them emotionally, intellectually, and sometimes even physically.

Sometimes, you might be able to help them change external circumstances, such as referring them to a new resource in their job search or offering to counsel them and their significant other in couple's therapy.

Whether a client's suicidal ideation is related to external circumstances or is a result of internal feelings of depression, hopelessness, or anxiety, your role will mostly be to help them address their feelings and develop new coping skills to deal with them more effectively. This can reduce their level of risk for future suicide attempts.

ASSESS FOR RISK

My basic questions change. I already know they've been having thoughts of suicide, so I ask them how intense their suicidal feelings are right now. I follow that up with more questions.

» **DO YOU THINK YOU MIGHT MAKE ANOTHER ATTEMPT?**

Timing is everything. While you want to gather this information, check your pacing so you don't overwhelm your client.

As for the question of whether a client thinks they might make another attempt, responses can vary.

"No, because I realized I really did not want to die. I just want my problems to go away."

"I don't know. Maybe. I'm not really sure."

"Nothing has changed so, yeah, I think I probably would."

This question can clarify a client's risk level so you can decide on a point of intervention. It is also helpful to review the circumstances surrounding their most recent attempt, which can aid you in evaluating if there is any risk for future attempts.

» **UNDER WHAT CIRCUMSTANCES DO YOU THINK THAT MIGHT HAPPEN?**

The feelings of hopelessness, helplessness, and worthlessness are invariably behind most suicide attempts. The predictability of another attempt is tempered by a client's current mood, the level of intensity of these three feelings, and their response to your attempts to intervene.

If, following an uncompleted attempt, nothing has changed, the odds of a person seeking help when they did not do so prior to their attempt are probably low. The fact that they are here with you now is a possible indication that their situation, outlook, and sense of hopelessness and helplessness have all changed. This can be a good thing in terms of reducing future risk. It is also something on which you can build during treatment.

» **WOULD YOU USE THE SAME METHOD OR A DIFFERENT ONE?**

Many clients, when talking about a possible subsequent attempt, will tell you that they will do it much differently next time. They may describe a method that carries a higher risk of lethality. Conversely, they may not have a specific method in mind but are clear about seeking out more lethal means. "The next time, I'm going to make sure I do it 'right.'"

» **DO YOU THINK YOU MIGHT TELL SOMEONE HOW YOU FEEL BEFORE YOU MAKE ANOTHER ATTEMPT?**

The fact that the client attempted suicide suggests that they either told no one about their plan, or they got no response or an inadequate one. Why, then, would they tell someone about their feelings the second time around if it didn't do any good before?

When I ask this question, clients often have the same response.

"Why would I? I tried to tell someone last time, and it did no good."

This is a point at which you might introduce the idea of a family session or some other modality that could involve the client's significant others. This assumes that such people are available and willing to participate. It also assumes that the client is agreeable to the idea.

12. THE CHALLENGE OF PROVIDING ONGOING TREATMENT

WE NOW HAVE assessment strategies and intervention techniques in the case of a suicide attempt. The next issue is how to prevent future attempts. While specific approaches can ensure a client's safety in the short-term, a long-term approach is meant to address and resolve whatever issues created the suicidal crisis in the first place.

Think of suicide as a symptom of a much larger problem. Unlike other disorders, such as alcoholism, which is seen as the problem in and of itself, albeit with other related problems, suicide is not viewed this way.

That's why, beyond the short-term challenge of how to intervene in a suicidal crisis to prevent a death, long-term issues require us to address why someone had become suicidal and to devise an appropriate treatment program.

I recognize two schools of thought on this. Crisis interventionists and crisis theory contends that by helping an individual successfully resolve a crisis, they will be better able to deal with the next crisis. Having studied crisis theory and trained countless professionals in crisis intervention, it would be contradictory for me to disagree with this premise.

There is certainly a great deal of legitimacy to the belief that a successful resolution of a crisis will better equip a person to deal with other crises. However, this does not imply that even the staunchest of crisis theorists and practitioners believe there is no need for ongoing treatment after the crisis has been stabilized and resolved.

When working with a suicidal individual, your first and foremost task is to help the client find stability and get to the point where they are no longer at risk (or at a much lower risk) for suicide. Once you reach that point, your work is not done. Yes, developing coping skills around a crisis can help, but the other school says that ongoing treatment is crucial and should be started as soon as possible.

The belief is that by addressing the issues that led a client to the point of becoming suicidal, you can begin to reduce the likelihood of another suicidal crisis. Simply stabilizing the situation and not addressing the broader issues will almost guarantee that a client's suicidal ideation will recur, usually sooner than later. The faster a client receives help, the less likely they are to become suicidal again.

Not everyone will be able to do the work that is necessary to deal with their problems. Many clients are more crisis oriented and do not see the need for ongoing treatment. Once they are past the crisis, they believe they will be fine.

Not so fast! We can almost predict that such a client will again find themselves in a crisis and/or suicidal state. Sometimes, I have told this to a client, predicting that they will probably experience another crisis sooner rather than later, unless they continue treatment.

While resistant clients may be frustrating, we must accept the precept that they have the right to refuse services—unless they are at imminent risk of harming themselves or someone else. All we can do is present our professional recommendations and let the client decide.

So, even when ongoing treatment is indicated for a depressed and suicidal client, not everyone will comply with your recommendation. Sometimes it's because a crisis has been resolved, and all is well. Sometimes a client's depression reinforces a defeatist feeling that nothing will help. Sometimes it's a lack of understanding of how depression can take over every aspect of one's life, even to the point of denying the need for ongoing treatment. That's where simple education can help, and all you can do is offer your services and hope for the best.

WHAT ABOUT MEDS?

I want to discuss the use of antidepressant medications. I am certainly a proponent of them when indicated, and I have seen their use, along with talking therapy, to have a tremendously positive effect.

The only caveat is that it takes time for medications to take effect. This is often difficult for clients to understand because they are looking for a quick fix.

I always try to explain this delayed effect to a client, especially because they need to take the medication as prescribed for it to take effect. I would hope and assume that the prescriber would have explained this as well, but I can never be sure.

It is also important that clients understand that even if they feel better, they need to continue their meds. Many clients will stop taking their meds, believing their depression has been "cured."

Once a client stops taking their medication and the depression sets in again, as is usually the case, hopefully, they will understand the need for staying on the medication. There may be a point where they can be weaned off it, but that will be up to their prescriber and them to decide.

So, here we are. Plenty to think about before we move on to related issues that should prove helpful for you.

13. EMOTIONAL LANDMINES

WE KNOW THAT most depressed, suicidal people experience three major feelings: hopelessness, helplessness, and worthlessness. While chapter 2 describes these major emotional states and addresses their presence and how they might originate, let's now examine what we can do to address those feelings and how we can deal with them as part of an overall intervention strategy.

Addressing these feelings in the context of a client's suicidal ideation will help alleviate the ideation while providing you with an opening to explore what brought them to this point in the first place.

SUICIDE IS A SYMPTOM

We have discussed how suicide is usually a symptom of a problem or situation. Suicidal ideation is a symptom. Think of suicide as a possible way to end a problem or situation, short- or long-term, that a client has been unable to manage successfully.

In any suicide-related intervention, your initial goal is stabilization. You must first take whatever steps seem necessary and appropriate to ensure a client's safety. The faster you can stabilize the situation and help the person reduce their level of suicidal ideation, the more likely you can help them find solutions to the problem(s) that led them to feeling suicidal.

In a previous section, we talked about the dynamics of suicidal feelings being temporary and the ambivalence regarding suicidal feelings. We discussed specific intervention strategies regarding those dynamics. The next intervention strategy is to explore the associated feelings that we talked about and how someone is affected by them.

HOPELESSNESS

As discussed earlier, hopelessness occurs when a person feels like they have tried everything to cope with their situation but to no avail. Your role then is to help them recognize that despite this feeling, there is hope.

Most everyone has experienced periods when they felt good because their life was going well. One intervention strategy with a client is to revisit the last time they felt okay. How long ago was it? What did it feel like? These questions will help them remember the good times.

This approach is meant to provide perspective on their life situation and help them understand that things can improve. Reflect on those positive times to remind them things can change for the better.

Your choice of words is vital. There is a big difference between *can* get better and *will* get better. You cannot predict with any certainty that a client *will* feel better. However, you can plant the idea that things *could* improve. This approach is known as an installation of hope, and the goal is to give that person, even in a small way, a sense that things may not be as hopeless as they think.

The next step is to set short-term, immediate goals and explore concrete ways to help that person feel better. It is important to make this process a "we" thing, as in "Let's see what we can do together that might help you feel better," or "Let's explore how we can work together and create options you might not have considered."

Don't make promises you cannot keep. Don't put yourself in a situation where you commit to doing anything that is beyond the scope of your role as the helper.

Of course, when exploring a time when someone felt better, there's always one person who will respond by saying that things were never good and that they can't remember a time when they didn't feel terrible. Obviously, this is a more difficult situation. In that case, my approach would be something like "Does that mean it is always going to be that way?" Analogies are a good tool: "Just because it's been cloudy all week, does that mean the sun will never come out again?"

Remember, resistance comes in many forms, and the person here is probably responding more as a function of their depression. There may also possibly be some type of memory impairment. Keep in mind who you are talking to. For example, adolescents tend to live more in the present. They also have a different sense of time. A young person may find it difficult to remember a time when they felt good and may come to believe they have always felt this bad, even if it has only been a few days.

HELPLESSNESS

A person suffering from depression typically has a narrow view of the world and of themselves. As described earlier, experiencing tunnel vision will also inhibit a person's ability to find solutions and alternative ways of dealing with their situation and feelings.

A depressed and suicidal individual typically sees themselves as having tried everything to make their life better with no success. They are at their wits end, unable to do anything on their own to feel better.

Your role is to help them find new ways to cope. First, it is important to explore what they have tried. Has anything worked, or has everything they've tried failed? You don't want to rehash old ground.

At this point, some clients will call into question your ability to help them, especially when they believe that nothing has worked and that you are both helpless to do anything. Again, this is a function of their depression. Clients can, and sometimes will, project their own feelings of helplessness onto you. It is also a function of the hopelessness they may be experiencing.

This is a cycle that keeps repeating itself. I feel helpless, therefore my situation is hopeless. Since there is no hope, there is no help, and I feel hopeless about being helpless, and on and on.

Clients will sometimes want to know what experience you have with someone like them. They will ask about your credentials and if you've ever dealt with anyone like them. They will ask how successful you have been working with people with depression who are prone to suicide. This is not as much about them questioning your ability as it is about the client (without saying so outright) asking their own potentially life-saving question: "What makes you think you can help me when I can't even help myself?"

This is actually a legitimate question regarding your training and experience. Clients have the right to know about these things. If you had cancer, you would want to know what credentials your oncologist processes and what experience they have in treating your illness.

Interns and providers who are new to the field may struggle with this question. There is an ongoing debate as to whether an intern, for example, should disclose that information to their clients from the start. I believe that this is best dealt with in an open and honest manner with the client.

Supervision is key, and it's not unheard of for one's supervisor to sit in on a session or two until the client feels comfortable working with the intern. If this is not an option, or if the client expresses a desire to see a more experienced provider, such a request should be honored.

The other question that is often posed by a client is whether their provider has ever felt suicidal: "How can you know what I'm going through and how I feel if you've never experienced it yourself?"

Let's refer to my question about the oncologist. Do I need to know if they have had cancer? No. Do I need to know what their training and experience is in treating my cancer? Absolutely!

The same is true in this situation. I do not have to have been suicidal to know how to help someone struggling with ideation. But I *do* need to explain to the client how my own training and experience has prepared me to be able to work with them in an effective manner.

The last thing I want to do is to allow the client's sense of helplessness to affect me in a similar way. I want to maintain my position as an explorer and coach. I want the client to join me in discovering ways that they may not have considered to alleviate their feelings of helplessness.

Here we go again, entering the realm of "we." Interventions to address feelings of helplessness should center around the idea of exploring together what options and strategies we might come up with to help. Of course, there must be a willingness on the client's part to listen to your ideas and be an active participant.

Dependency issues also need to be attended to. Some clients are so helpless, they are at a point of being almost totally immobilized. In these situations, a certain amount of symbolic hand-holding is not only acceptable but often necessary to help a person explore alternative ways of dealing with their depression and suicidal ideation. As we have discussed before, crisis theory, as it applies here, basically says that addressing these early dependency needs will provide a foundation for the client to eventually function on their own.

There are also situations where feelings of helplessness and hopelessness are so overwhelming, and the suicidal ideation is so strong, you may have to take charge. This might include an involuntary hospitalization or some other form of intervention that imposes controls over the client to prevent them from acting on their suicidal feelings. When and how you choose to use these strategies is subjective, but there are times when you may need to do so.

I saw a young woman for an initial evaluation who presented with severe symptoms of depression. She did not admit to any suicidal ideation, which I chose to believe based on her presentation and history. She was, however, so depressed as to be almost incapacitated.

We discussed possible ways of dealing with her depression, but none seemed to fit. She lived alone and did not want to go home to an empty apartment. She had no friends. Her family could not understand how or why she was so depressed. Thankfully, however, they had enough insight to realize she needed help, and her mother had actually arranged for her appointment with me.

This was one of the most debilitating examples of depression I had ever come across. I concluded that this client would probably benefit from a short stay at the inpatient facility that my agency managed, where she could receive a much more intensive treatment regimen than I could offer. A course of antidepressant medication could also begin there.

As I discussed this option with my client, she could not come to any conclusions regarding my recommendations. I finally asked her if she was having a hard time making decisions. This is often an issue for anyone who is severely depressed.

"I can't even decide what to have for breakfast!" she lamented.

Hearing that, and based on my assessment of her condition, I asked her if she would accept my recommendation that she admit herself to the inpatient facility.

"If that is what you think," she answered, though somewhat reluctantly.

My response was simple. "I think that is what we need to do," I said, making it a *we* thing.

The look of relief on my client's face was remarkable. It was as though the weight that had been burdening her was lifted, even if in a small way.

With her permission, I invited her mother, who had accompanied her and was in the waiting room, to join the session. I explained the situation to her, including her daughter's acceptance of my recommendations. Her daughter was admitted that same day.

Of course, this is not always how things work. This was a case where the client's level of hopelessness and helplessness was so profound that I felt justified in taking this approach. Had she refused to accept my recommendation, would I have taken steps to have her hospitalized involuntarily? That's a tough question.

While she was further in the depths of depression than anyone I had seen up until then, she denied any suicidal ideation. She was not a danger to others, and she could meet her basic needs, even though she did report having difficulty in this area.

The fact is, when this client agreed with my suggestion, it was as much of a relief for me as it appeared to be for her.

So, when and how is it appropriate for providers to intervene in such a way? There is no hard-and-fast answer, but consider this: We practice in an era where treatment goals and modalities are more client and/or family driven than ever. Client and family voice and choice is a philosophy that has been adopted by many agencies and programs, especially by those who provide services for children and families.

The rationale is to empower families and allow them to be in control of their treatment. While I share this belief, I also think there are times when we must make the hard decisions that a client cannot. The case I've described here is a good example.

Doctors are much better at this. We give them almost carte blanche when it comes to diagnosis and treatment. And why wouldn't we? They are, after all, the experts. This concept is called Aesculapian authority:

> "This awesome authority, which rules out any patient participation in the decision-making process, stems from a three-pronged power base: the physician's expertise, the patient's faith in him, and the belief that he has almost mystical powers."[4]

Even in the medical professions, this unquestioned authority is waning, albeit somewhat reluctantly in some circles. Let's face it. There are times when we are more than happy, and rightly so, to let a doctor make decisions on our behalf.

So, here's my point. There are times when we, as providers of mental health services, can and should take control of a situation. How and when to do so is subjective, but training and experience are your best tools when making this determination.

You will probably not encounter a situation like the one I described very often, but there may be a time when taking charge is the best and only way to go. Once again, it's important to make it a "we" thing as

---

[4]—Kalisch BJ. Of half gods and mortals: Aesculapian authority. *Nursing Outlook*. (1975) 23:22–8

much as possible. For example, "Let's think about what we can do to help you," or "Here's what I think we should do."

It's amazing what using the right pronoun can do.

WORTHLESSNESS

Most depressed, suicidal people do not like themselves. I have repeatedly heard, "The world would be better off without me," or "No one will miss me when I'm gone."

Poor self-esteem is a difficult issue to deal with in any situation, but it is even more challenging when someone feels that their death would be a good thing for their family and friends. When I face someone who believes this, I respond empathically with statements like "I understand how you must feel and how easy it must be for you to accept the idea that everyone would actually be better off without you."

Once I have established that I understand how they are feeling, I am able to confront, in a supportive manner, the false beliefs they have about themselves. I try asking, "Do you really believe that no one will miss you?" or "You truly believe your family will be better off without you?" At this point, most clients know where I am going. Their response says that even though they may feel that way, they don't really want to believe it.

Others respond by saying yes, they believe that everyone would be better off without them, particularly their family. My response is to ask if they have ever checked it out with their family. Usually, a client has not, and they assume, based on how they feel about themselves, that this must be the case. If possible, I suggest that we bring the family in to ask them.

Trial attorneys have a rule: Don't ask questions if you do not already know the answer. So, before I bring the family in to meet with the client, I might have a brief conversation with them in private to check out what their response is going to be.

Though rare, there have been occasions where the family has

agreed, saying they do believe they would be better off without the client. Oftentimes, these feelings exist because the family has been dealing with the client and their feelings of depression and suicide for a long time, and they are simply exhausted. I have had family members tell me they wish the client would just go ahead and do it so they could move on.

While this is not a response that I would like a client to hear, there are ways to work with this and still get a positive result. Understanding the family's feelings of frustration and their own helplessness and helping them communicate these feelings to the client can open a large door to facilitate more discussion.

This usually results in the family acknowledging that they want the client to get better, but they are at their wits end as to how to help them get there. This is a perfect opportunity to bring the family and client together to explore solutions that involve everyone in the process.

The more preferred response by the family is when they tell the client that they would not be better off without them. Most families respond in this manner, which provides an opportunity for a positive intervention that involves everyone.

So, when it comes to helping people work through their feelings of hopelessness, helplessness, and worthlessness, well, it does take a village . . .

SELF-PUNISHMENT AND ANGER

Suicidal behavior and suicide attempts are often used as a form of self-punishment. A sense of worthlessness and low self-esteem contribute to this dynamic. Though I have seen this in a general population of suicidal clients, it seems to occur more often among adolescents.

Teenagers are not always good at expressing anger in a healthy way. They often feel as if doing so is not allowed in any shape or form. It is sometimes much easier for a young person to internalize this anger and take it out on themselves in a self-destructive way.

Internalized feelings of anger, coupled with an underlying

depression and feelings of low self-esteem, can contribute to and provide enough motivation for a serious suicide attempt. Whether you are working with someone who expresses suicidal ideation or a client who has made a suicide attempt, it is important to explore how anger may have contributed to those feelings and their attempt.

Why might a client report that their suicidal feelings or attempt was a result of feeling anger toward someone else? Most of the time, the reasons fall into one of two categories. The first is the familiar idea of revenge or getting back at someone who wronged them in some way. The second relates to the client's inability or unwillingness to express anger toward others, that it is easier to take out those feelings on themselves.

There may be reality-based reasons for why a client cannot or should not express their anger toward another person without running the risk of some consequence. Expressing anger toward a teacher, supervisor, or even a parent can sometimes create more problems for the person. If that is the case, there are ways to help a client understand and learn how to deal with their anger in a healthy manner and to teach them why internalizing that anger serves no useful purpose.

Those situations notwithstanding, it is also important to understand why a client deals with their anger in a self-destructive manner. In that situation, I ask them why they would choose to take out that anger on themselves. The most common answer is that it's just easier.

I usually respond with something like "So, let me get this straight. It's easier for you to take your anger and turn it inward than it is to express your anger outward." My next statement is meant to be provocative. "You really think that little of yourself that it's easier to punish yourself for something someone else did or said to you."

By pointing these things out to the client, I hope to help them understand how their feelings of worthlessness might also contribute to their suicidal ideation. I am in no way suggesting that by developing an awareness of their own feelings of worthlessness that they will then decide to turn their anger outward and become homicidal. A bit extreme, but hopefully you get my point.

In general, by acknowledging the existence of these feelings, including the presence of anger and low self-esteem, the client and I can begin to explore where these feelings come from and how they contribute to their suicidal feelings. Getting someone to feel better about themselves is one step in the process of decreasing their suicidal ideation. Helping a client improve their self-esteem, develop better coping skills, and envision a more positive future are all strategies to address their feelings of hopelessness, helplessness, and worthlessness.

RAGE

From a psychodynamic standpoint, we must explore feelings of rage. Primitive rage, though experienced at a subconscious or preconscious level, can be so intense that it overpowers any other feelings a person may be experiencing.

One of the first parts of the human brain to have been developed over the millennium is the limbic system. This central core is where certain primitive drives and emotions lie. Rage is one of these emotions.

Rage is more than just anger. It can be so all-encompassing that it creates an almost frightening belief that expressing it would destroy the person and everyone and everything around them. In these circumstances, committing suicide, in the client's mind, is a way of "protecting" the world around them from that rage.

From a conscious standpoint, this could be the source of a client's belief that everyone would be better off without them. The challenge is to understand where this belief is rooted.

This is difficult because, for the most part, rage is an unconscious process and not something you will get close to addressing in the short-term. These feelings and other associated behaviors are often indicators of a more deep-rooted personality disorder. Initially, the best you can hope for is to stabilize the immediate situation and get the client involved in long-term, ongoing psychotherapy.

TRAUMA

Past or recent trauma can be a major contributor to someone's suicidal ideation. In the short-term, you are not going to address a client's trauma history and its effects, which can include feelings of rage, depression, low self-esteem, and self-blame. Your goal is to help the client understand and deal with their immediate situation. Follow-up services are crucial.

We are learning more and more about the effects of trauma on one's psychological and emotional makeup. There is also a body of research that examines the effects of trauma on brain development, especially among children and adolescents.

One thing we do know is that self-punishment, in whatever form, can be a symptom of post-traumatic stress disorder. Self-blame is often associated with the sense of being out of control and the frustration and anger associated with that sense.

At some point, a trauma history is important to assess. This can help you to gain a better understanding of the source of the anger and frustration that a client might express.

This subject is elusive, so I suggest you dig deeper into the wealth of published research and findings that are readily available.

One thing I want to point out is this: There is a difference between a diagnosis of post-traumatic stress disorder, PTSD, and acute stress disorder. The former applies only to situations where the event or events have occurred more than one month prior to the onset of symptoms. Acute stress disorder applies to situations where the symptoms appear within the first few days or month of the event or events.

We often hear television shows and movies use PTSD to describe a person's reaction to an event that has just occurred. I'll allow for a certain amount of dramatic license, but it's more than just a pet peeve of mine. I have seen clinicians who have used this diagnosis incorrectly as well.

The complication is that the approach to treatment can be very different. In cases of acute stress disorder, the traumatic event is usually more readily identifiable. This allows for a more direct, reality-based examination of the event(s) and its effect on the client. Often, a more crisis-oriented approach is indicated. This is especially true in cases where the client was functioning relatively well prior to the trauma.

Treating PTSD is much more complicated. The traumatic event(s) may not be as evident and may have occurred much further in the client's past. Childhood trauma is a good example. The client may have locked their experience deep into their unconscious until a trigger of some sort brings it back into their conscious awareness. In those cases, half the battle is trying to identify what the trauma was.

In either case, the symptomatology can be very similar.

14. CONTRACTING FOR SAFETY

CONTRACTING FOR SAFETY, also known as "no-suicide contracts," is a technique that is often used as a strategy when intervening with someone expressing suicidal ideation. While a no-suicide contract can be an effective tool, certain things about them are important to understand when it comes to when and how to use them.

a. A no-suicide contract is a Band-Aid. It is not meant to be a long-term solution to a person's problems. It is simply meant to buy time.
b. A no-suicide contract is a delay tactic. It may or may not prevent a person from ultimately attempting suicide, but it may give you time to intervene and reduce the level of risk.
c. A no-suicide contract is one of many tools that can be used in the prevention of suicide. It cannot and should not be used in isolation or to the exclusion of other intervention strategies.
d. A no-suicide contract is a concrete means to an end. Its goal is to allow a client the option of putting off their suicide attempt for a specific amount of time. It gives a provider time to address their client's suicidal feelings and hopefully reduce or eliminate the level of risk.
e. No-suicide contracts are overused. There are circumstances when contracting for safety can be used appropriately, but it is also a strategy that is often utilized as a blanket intervention with every client who expresses suicidal ideation

I have lost count of how many times a client made a suicide attempt and the provider's response was "But we had a contract!" Well, yeah! So, what are you going to do, sue the client for breach of contract?

TYPES OF CONTRACTS

We use two basic types of contracts: verbal and written. I tend to use verbal contracts, which can be effective if you follow certain guidelines.

VERBAL CONTRACTS

When making a verbal contract, your role is to lay the groundwork for what you are asking your client to say. It is not for you to say the words for the client and ask them to agree. In other words, I would not say, "Promise me that for the next twenty-four hours, you will not make a suicide attempt" and simply have them answer, "Okay."

I believe that it is important for the client to say the words. Having them hear their own voice as they promise not to make a suicide attempt for whatever specified amount of time you have agreed to makes it more real for the client. It tends to create a stronger sense of commitment on their part.

Eye contact is important when making a verbal contract. I not only ask a client to make a no-suicide statement, but I also insist that they look me straight in the eye while doing so. Just like saying the words, there is something about eye contact that creates a stronger sense of commitment by the client.

We touched upon the issue of cultural factors in relation to suicide, but the issue of eye contact is worth mentioning. A few years ago, I presented my suicide prevention workshop at a national convention on crisis intervention. There were people there from all over the country.

When I spoke about eye contact and verbal no-suicide contracts, a small group of participants raised their hands in unison. One person in the group told me they worked in a community where many of their clients were Native American. In that culture, they explained, eye contact with a White person was not something that was typically done.

"They won't look me in the eye," she said, "especially when we first meet."

Culture is an important factor in everything we do, and this was a glaring example of how a client's culture can have a direct effect on a specific intervention strategy. Like anything you do, certain factors will influence how a client reacts. Their cultural, ethnic, racial, religious, and demographic characteristics will play an important role in this process.

WRITTEN CONTRACTS

The best written no-suicide contract I've ever seen was done by a clinician with a seventeen-year-old client and her parents.

The client, a high school senior, was brought in by her parents for an initial session because of what they had identified as signs of depression. Their daughter was not eating well, not sleeping, disinterested in everything, and constantly sad.

During the interview, the client reported that she had been having thoughts of suicide. She had planned to take an overdose of pills but had no specifics about when, where, or how she was going to do this. She also reported that she had no access to medications.

Everyone in the session responded appropriately to the client's reported suicidal feelings. Her parents, the clinician, and the client all expressed concern about her safety. While the young woman appeared to be at risk, the clinician did not feel that hospitalization was indicated.

There was, however, an obvious need to take some immediate action. Despite their willingness to cooperate, determining what that action should be seemed to baffle the family.

The clinician introduced the idea of making a contract. She explained that it was a concrete way of dealing with the immediacy of the situation and getting through the weekend.

Though initially reluctant, the client agreed to a contract if she could have certain things written into it. The result was a written contract that contained every component one could hope for in this type of document:

1) A firm commitment by the client that she would not make a suicide attempt during the terms of the contract.
2) A realistic time frame agreed to by all parties, which was the entire weekend.
3) Positive, planned activities that the client and parents agreed to, which also served as a distraction for the client so she would not spend the weekend ruminating in her room.
4) Realistic commitments by everyone involved, including the clinician, who agreed to accept a phone call from the client as a check-in. The clinic program was structured so that the clinician could receive a phone call from the client over the weekend.

If you find yourself in similar circumstances, it's important that you not make promises you cannot keep. For example, if taking a phone call from a client is not possible, do not make that commitment. However, if a twenty-four-hour crisis line is available, you might suggest that the client use that as a resource if she feels it is necessary.

The contract also included family/friend involvement. This is important because it brings other people into the process. In this case, the parents agreed to let their daughter go to an activity on Saturday with her boyfriend. She agreed to check in with them while she was out.

Even though the client was not particularly interested in religion, she agreed to attend church with her parents on Sunday. This was something the parents requested to include in the contract. Their daughter's willingness to comply said a lot about her commitment to the process and her ability to see things from her parents' perspective.

A safety plan was put in place in case the client had a crisis over the weekend. The client also agreed to inform her parents and visit an emergency services program or the hospital emergency department if she began to feel suicidal.

A follow-up appointment with the clinician on Monday was incorporated into the contract.

An additional component stated that the client would begin working with the clinician to address her concerns that had led to her feeling suicidal. This is a good example of the need to address the underlying problems as soon as possible as a way of preventing any future suicidal ideation or attempts.

Signatures are an important component of any written contract. Everyone who was involved in this process signed the contract and got a copy. The original was placed in the client's chart.

This contract proved to be effective in getting the client and her parents through the weekend and set the stage for the client to begin working on the issues that brought her to that point. For several years, I continued to use this example in my training seminars.

Obviously, not every written contract or verbal agreement works this well. Contracting taps almost directly into a client's ambivalence about wanting to live or die. It also addresses the temporary nature of suicidal feelings by buying time and giving a client something positive to hold onto. Usually, the more time you buy, the less suicidal a person will be at the end of the contract.

As a side note, I've never figured out why it always seems that if a crisis is going to occur, it will happen after 3 p.m. on a Friday. Maybe it's because everyone is getting ready to go home for the weekend. Maybe there's an underlying sense of desperation that "If I don't deal with this now, I'll be stuck with it all weekend." I don't know, but it happens a lot.

As I mentioned above, we also see circumstances when no-suicide contracts do not work. We can usually pinpoint specific reasons for why that occurs. Understanding the limits of a contract is important.

WHAT NO-SUICIDE CONTRACTS ARE NOT

A no-suicide contract is not a panacea. Contracting for safety does not solve all your problems or those of a client, and it does not work in every situation.

Contracting for safety means you are getting a person to agree to not make a suicide attempt for a specific period. It does not mean that you do not have to begin, as soon as possible, to address the issues related to a person's suicide and the circumstances that brought them to that point.

Suicide contracts are not the end-all. They are a delay tactic, and at that point, your work has only just begun.

So, when and how can you and should you use a no-suicide contract effectively? This is a difficult question to answer because it relies heavily on a client's circumstances and their provider's experience, judgment, and assessment of the situation.

I tend to use contracts judiciously and usually only when I feel that I have not been able to address a client's suicidal ideation or help get them to a point where we both believe that they are at a substantially lower risk.

This is a good time to, once again, talk about resistance. Just because someone presents themselves to you as being open to help, that may not actually be the case. Sometimes, a client is coerced into seeking help by a parent, a spouse, or the court system. Even when clients come in of their own free will, they are often skeptical and doubt your ability to help them, let alone believe in their own ability and/or willingness to change.

It's a conundrum. If a client believes they cannot be helped, why will they bother seeing you in the first place? The simple answer is, at some level, they acknowledge that they have a problem that requires outside intervention.

As I have said before, for a depressed and suicidal client, resistance is often a function of their depression. In that case, resistance is also an outward manifestation of a client's feelings of hopelessness, helplessness, and worthlessness.

Clients in this state often give out a double message. "Help me, but I'm going to make it very difficult for you to do so." Understanding the origins of this resistance and the dynamics behind it will give you some insight as to where and how you choose to intervene.

Contracting for safety becomes what I refer to as "a process intervention." After gathering all the information, I need to assess a client's current situation and level of risk. The next step is to work with the client to address some of these issues to at least reduce any imminent risk of harm.

There are times, however, where, despite our best efforts, a client is not able to begin the work that needs to be done to resolve their issues. They become fixated on the present and cannot get past their suicidal feelings.

Depending on the level of risk and the severity of the situation, you might choose to employ strategies, such as involuntary hospitalization and contacting family members. This is when I might consider using a no-suicide contract. This is also when your clinical judgment and experience must come into play.

Keeping all of this in mind, a no-suicide contract may not be an effective strategy for the following reasons.

APATHY

We must always try to understand how depression affects our clients. Apathy is often a function of depression. A client reaches a point where they just don't care. They see no end to their depression and no hope for themselves, so why would they consider making a contract with you for their own safety?

UNREALISTIC EXPECTATIONS

The most common unrealistic expectation that can cause a client to become resistant to contracting is related to the length of time you may be requesting. In most cases, a week is much too long. For some, even a day can be too much. This becomes a negotiating point for you and your client, and hopefully they can agree on a reasonable amount of time to not attempt suicide.

WHEN A PERSON REALLY WANTS TO DIE

Some clients are not able to agree to a contract because their suicidal ideation is so strong and resolute that they have every intention of killing themselves. In these circumstances, contracting will not work, and you will have to take other steps to assure the client's safety.

DEPRESSION AND DECISION-MAKING ABILITIES

As we know, depression often interferes with a client's ability to make decisions. This is not classic resistance. It's more a function of depression, and you may be asking too much for a client who is emotionally incapable of agreeing to anything at that time.

LACK OF TRUST

This is especially true in situations where you are seeing a client for the first time. They do not know you. No relationship has been established, and there is no reason for the client to trust you. How you gain a client's trust in such a short period of time and how you get them to accept the idea that you have their best interests at heart is up to you, but trust is crucial to the success or failure of any intervention, much less a no-suicide contract.

CULTURAL FACTORS

We discussed how this affects verbal contracts with respect to eye contact, etc., but cultural factors also come into play with written contracts. This is not to say that cultural factors always inhibit the process. There may be situations where it helps. It is important to understand that culture can play a role in both positive and negative ways.

Contracting for safety can be a powerful and effective tool if used appropriately. However, please keep in mind that it is only one tool in what should be a full toolbox.

15. "THE QUESTION" REVISITED

IN CHAPTER TEN, I asked a fundamental question: Do you believe that anyone has the right to commit suicide? Let's revisit that question now so you can come up with your own answer. This may touch a nerve and could affect how you choose to intervene.

This is a specific question about a specific set of circumstances, and how you feel about a client or situation will affect you, if you let it. Be aware of these feelings and understand how they might influence your approach, relationship, and even effectiveness with certain clients. Sometimes, interpreting these feelings for yourself can be useful and help you arrive at a diagnosis.

YOU AND YOUR FEELINGS

Personality disorders are difficult to diagnose accurately, and it usually takes time to reach such a conclusion. Of course, the criteria that the *DSM-5* describes can be useful, but there are other ways to arrive at a determination. When I'm faced with these circumstances, I rely partially on my own reaction to the person across from me.

Like any practitioner, I have my own issues with certain situations. Paying attention to those feelings is important. For example, if five minutes into meeting a new client, I want to shake them and say, "It's not always just about you," I am probably heading down the road of narcissistic personality disorder.

In another situation, a client might tell me they have been to six other therapists and that I might finally be the one who can succeed in helping them. If I respond, "I can rescue you. I can be the one to help you when no one else has been able to," then I'm probably in trouble and potentially coming face-to-face with a borderline personality.

Obviously, much more is required to arrive at a diagnosis, especially with a potential personality disorder. Your reactions and feelings toward your client can be a useful tool, but they are only part of a bigger equation.

Additionally, what you bring to any session, whether an initial diagnostic appointment or twenty meetings later, matters. The client doesn't care if you're having a bad day, and they shouldn't. If your last three sessions didn't go exactly as you had hoped, it should not matter to them. When you walk into a session, leave your stuff at the door. Focus on the needs of your client, not the fact that you didn't get the raise you were seeking.

THE QUESTION

Why is the question of whether a person has the right to commit suicide so important? Your answer will speak to how you feel about this issue and how it might affect your approach with a client. So, what do you think?

Do you object to the idea of one's right based on an ethical or religious belief? Have you had an experience with a loved one that has affected your opinion? Are you an advocate of client rights in relation to any issue, much less their right to die?

Your feelings and your answer to the question will be affected by these personal experiences and your own values and beliefs.

Answering the question from a more clinical perspective is another matter altogether. Has your "professional self" and what you already know and believe helped you develop your answer? Has anything I have provided here made a difference or served to reinforce your thinking? A combination of personal feelings, training, and experience will help you decide on an answer. No matter what your answer may be, as I said before, leave your feelings at the door.

MY ANSWER

Do I think people have the right to commit suicide? Yes, but not if I'm around. As contradictory as that may sound, let me explain. I believe that anyone has the right to take their own life, but when I can intervene, I will do whatever I can to prevent that from happening.

My reasoning is based on the two concepts we have previously discussed. If I accept, as I do, the premise that suicidal feelings are temporary and that, regardless of the intensity of your client's ideation, there is always a level of ambivalence, it becomes almost incumbent upon me to intervene.

That said, even our best efforts cannot stop someone from committing suicide, if they are determined enough. Answering the question, however, will at least provide you with some insight and awareness as to how you will approach a suicidal crisis.

PART FIVE:

PREVENTION

16. THE ROLE OF TRADITIONAL MEDIA

WHEN IT COMES to suicide and prevention, the debate about the role of media continues, including how people are affected in negative and positive ways by media reports of suicide.

For example, are certain populations—adolescents, people with severe mental disorders, and emotionally vulnerable individuals—more influenced by the media? I think so, but I am not an expert in this field. That said, it's clear that in this era of access to instant information, the potential for someone to be influenced by online content and a twenty-four-hour news cycle is greater than it has ever been.

We have seen how the media has covered this inappropriately in the past. I don't believe that such coverage would drive someone to make a suicide attempt, but it certainly wouldn't help.

Years ago, an adolescent girl and boy committed suicide together. Sitting in the front seat of the girl's family car, with the garage door closed, they ran a hose from the exhaust pipe through the front window, started the engine, and died of carbon monoxide poisoning.

A local television news program decided to report on it. They sent a video crew to the home with a reporter who speculated on-air that this was a suicide pact, a *Romeo and Juliet* scenario, because the parents did not approve of the relationship. At the end, the camera panned to the interior of the car and zoomed in on a flower that the couple had left on the dashboard.

I cannot blame the TV station entirely because, at the time, there was little discussion or writing about the role of media in relation to suicide and prevention. But this story could not have been handled any worse.

There was no follow-up at that station. No experts were brought in to discuss suicide prevention strategies or warning signs to educate the public, especially parents.

More importantly, no one framed this event as preventable or explained that suicide is not an acceptable answer to one's problems. Instead, the story was presented in a highly romanticized fashion that turned it into something akin to a Greek tragedy.

We know that the media has a responsibility to report the news. Understanding that adolescents are especially susceptible to suggestion makes it just as important to not only report these events as news but to present the story objectively instead of sensationalizing it.

Media should be responsible for presenting information about the warning signs of suicide, along with preventative steps that parents and educators can take. Media outlets can also provide resource information, such as a listing of local mental health providers and contact information for a local crisis line, if one exists in their community, and any other relevant resources.

The contact number of the National Suicide Prevention Lifeline has been revised to a much simpler number: 988. This is a big step in improving accessibility to a much-needed resource. Information like this cannot be overemphasized.

Thankfully, we have come a long way over the last few years. Most local and national media outlets have become sensitive to the potential impact that stories about suicide, and particularly adolescent suicides, can have on others. They have become very careful about how these stories are being reported. For the most part, they understand the need to provide as much information as possible, including the 988 number.

There will continue to be media outlets that choose to sensationalize stories of suicide. This is especially true in cases of a celebrity suicide. Fortunately, those stations and websites are becoming more of a minority, and we now see more media opting to educate the public.

17. SOCIAL MEDIA

WHEN IT COMES to the role social media plays in our lives, we cannot underestimate its impact, especially in relation to how it can affect vulnerable individuals and groups who are active on sites like Facebook, Instagram, TikTok, and Twitter, now X. We tend to vilify these sites as major contributors to reinforcing negative stereotypes, platforms for cyberbullying, a place for misinformation, and other negative and potentially harmful postings.

Social media can serve a useful purpose. For example, consider someone who is housebound for whatever reason. Having contact with friends and family through social media can be a good thing because it can ease feelings of isolation, which can often exacerbate preexisting feelings of hopelessness, helplessness, and worthlessness.

Sadly, the flip side is just as prevalent. The misuse of what probably started out as a seemingly harmless way of sharing our lives with others has raised concerns in many circles, including the federal government.

RISK AND REWARD

Does social media contribute to suicide risk? If so, how, and why does this occur?

One of the most vulnerable stages of our life cycle is adolescence. It's when we are most unsure of ourselves, a time when change comes in waves, and not always for the better.

An adolescent's self-image and self-esteem can be held hostage by a variety of influences. Negative feelings about oneself can be triggered by social media, where young people typically spend a great deal of time. Some adolescents become obsessed with their online profiles and the minute-by-minute postings that appear on their sites.

We have seen numerous cases of adolescents making disparaging remarks online about their peers. Kids gang up on each other, sometimes even suggesting their targets kill themselves.

Can we say with certainty that this can cause someone to commit suicide? While online harassment may not be enough, it can certainly contribute. While there are positive, helpful comments out there, where kids actually feel supported, it seems the negative is more the norm, which can have adverse effects on vulnerable children.

THE PERILS OF BULLYING

Bullying is common among adolescents, as victims and perpetrators. Most bullies act out as a way of overcompensating for their own shortcomings. *Do unto others before they do unto you.* Confront a bully, and they will often back down. This isn't always the case because some people are just plain mean.

Adolescents have their own way of zeroing in on others' vulnerabilities, especially peers. A bully can sense "weakness" and those who are easily influenced, which is a distinct trait during adolescence. Bullies often capitalize on this, mostly to mask their own feelings of inadequacy.

Social media is a potent outlet for this behavior. Posting online is safer than a direct confrontation. It can be done from a distance, even anonymously or under a false name. This is convenient for bullies, who are mostly cowards at heart.

The following is not so much a story of bullying but an example of how influential one person can be over another during this vulnerable developmental stage.

THE STORY OF CONRAD AND MICHELLE

Conrad Roy was an eighteen-year-old with a history of depression and social anxiety. Conrad met Michelle Carter in the summer of 2012. For the next two years, they had a few in-person get-togethers, but most of their interactions were via text messaging and emails.

On July 12, 2014, Conrad placed a small, gas-powered generator in the cab of his pickup truck. His intent was to commit suicide by carbon monoxide poisoning. While he was contemplating his death, Conrad and Michelle were actively texting.

Some months later, a review of Michelle's texts showed that she was encouraging Conrad to go through with his suicide. Several of Conrad's texts expressed his ambivalence about going through with it. Michelle responded by texting that he should go through with his suicide, which he finally did. She was subsequently tried and convicted of involuntary manslaughter. She served fifteen months in prison and was released on probation.

This case is not necessarily a typical example of cyberbullying. Apparently, Conrad was an active participant in debating his suicide with Michelle. However, this case does speak to the influence that texting and online posts can have on young people.

How do we address this issue?

Like anything related to an adolescent's daily life, the first step is for parents to be aware of what their child is seeing, reading, and even sending to others. You simply cannot "fix" what you don't know is "broken." Providers also need to expand their areas of assessment to include questions about their client's use of social media. This is true for anyone seeking our assistance, regardless of their age.

18. SUICIDE PREVENTION IN SCHOOLS

SEVERAL YEARS AGO, I was approached by a local high school district to discuss designing and implementing a suicide prevention education program. Three students in that district had committed suicide within a short period, and the director of the school psychology department was rattled.

"We are scared," he told me during that first meeting.

During the early 1980s, the rate of adolescent suicide in the United States had more than tripled. People called it an epidemic, and while no one could explain the cause, we saw agreement from experts across all disciplines that something needed to be done.

After meeting with key personnel from the school district, I agreed, with both enthusiasm and caution, to work with them to develop a model of prevention and education. Little was being done at the time to address this issue in a school setting, and even less had been written about effective approaches, so we were flying blind.

Up until then, I had provided crisis intervention training for various groups, including hotline volunteers and mental health practitioners. I had made presentations on suicide and suicide prevention in individual classrooms but had never done anything on such a large scale.

This was a large suburban high school district, with four campuses and more than 12,000 students. The goal was to educate and train all faculty and staff and to present a program to every student within the district. Needless to say, this was a huge undertaking.

THE PROCESS

We began by forming a committee of key district personnel whose task was to develop a comprehensive program of training and education of all faculty, staff, and students at each campus. We began in the spring and planned to have it all ready by the time school started again in September. If you think we were naive about the timeline, you would be right!

Educating and training the faculty and staff took much longer than anyone anticipated. We also had to reassure the district administration, school principals, etc., that while the training was a necessary component of the program, we were not expecting educators to assume the role of mental health professionals.

We were able to make a strong case for educating faculty and staff about the warning signs of suicide, using the rationale that teachers were especially in a position to identify a potentially troubled student. The training included information about the warning signs of suicide—a drop in grades, acting out, apathy, etc., that might be identified in the context of a classroom setting. We also discussed the steps that faculty and staff should take if they encountered a student whose behavior might be a cause for concern.

Each campus set up in-house crisis teams that received more focused training, including basic crisis intervention techniques. Most teams were staffed by school psychologists, counselors, and social workers. All of these individuals were generally well-versed in dealing with students who might be having an emotional crisis. Members of each team were identified to students, faculty, and staff at each school through various means.

Our next step was to present an educational program for every student in the district. We began with a general assembly for each class year.

After a brief introduction, we showed a film that discussed the warning signs of suicide, followed by comments from me and key people from the school, and a final question-and-answer period. Then individual classroom discussions were held, led by teachers, faculty, and staff specially trained to facilitate these discussions and answer questions.

During the planning process, we recognized that some students might have strong reactions to the program and that they might need individual intervention. School counselors, psychologists, and social workers were made available for students who requested help or were identified by someone else as needing assistance. The crisis teams were utilized for this purpose.

I'd be lying if I said the programs went entirely smoothly without any hiccups. Since there were hardly any precedents for this type of program, this was a learn-as-you-go endeavor.

TRIAL AND ERROR

The first assembly with the junior class at one of the schools did not start well, despite our best intentions. As the students entered the school theater, they were directed from the stage by the dean of students. "Find your seats as quickly as possible. We have a very long program today," he announced.

A recipe for disaster? You guessed right. There is no better way to lose a group of high school kids than telling them they're going to have to sit quietly for a "long" time.

We also had no idea that the dean had decided (on his own) to moderate the program and that he was probably the most disliked individual in the school and someone for whom the students had no respect. Far be it from me to cast aspersions on anyone, but the proof was in the pudding.

We also didn't know that this particular junior class was probably the most difficult one in the entire district. At an assembly a month earlier, they had all but booed and chased a speaker off the stage.

One segment of our program took a chapter from the Phil Donahue program, who had pioneered the concept of audience participation in a talk-show format. Phil would host an expert in a certain field or a celebrity and would spend the first half of the show in dialogue with them. The remainder of his program had him wander through the audience, taking questions directed at his guest(s).

We thought this was a great idea and decided that after the film and a brief presentation, we would take questions from students. Little did we know, we were opening Pandora's box.

By the time the second student stood up with a question, we were in the middle of a shouting match between the students and the dean about conditions at the school. A couple of other students said they felt insulted by the program.

"Why are you coming into our building with this bullshit?" one student challenged.

Things deteriorated from there. The dean halted the assembly and sent the students back to their classrooms.

We immediately met with the principal and administration to talk about what just happened. There was a strong consensus that we should not continue the program. To his credit, the head psychologist for the district argued that the program should continue but that we should make changes to avoid future problems.

From then on, we made sure that each school principal participated in the program. We also distributed cards to the students and asked them to write down any questions they might have.

In total, there were eleven more assemblies at three different schools and individual classroom discussions with every student in each building. As we adjusted on the fly, the program went much more smoothly and was generally considered successful.

We also held a parent education night at each campus. Attendance was spotty, but we felt it was important to provide as much education as possible and inform parents about the program we were providing for their children.

We also sent a letter to parents prior to each assembly. It described our goals and announced that if any parent did not want their child to participate, all they had to do was call the school.

The feedback we received from parents was generally positive. I can recall only one critical comment, and I'm not even sure that's the right way to describe it.

A parent of one child who attended "School A" called the principal at her child's school. She was very much in favor of the program and was glad we were providing it at School B because she knew that campus had many problems. She didn't think we needed to run the program at her child's school because, "Thank God, our campus doesn't have those kinds of problems!"

The choice to opt out of the program was also made available directly to students who might not wish to participate. Faculty and staff were asked to identify students they felt might have difficulty with the topic of suicide.

Individual meetings were held with these students, and they were allowed to decide if they wanted to participate. These students, as well as those whose parents did not want them to participate, were assigned to a classroom that essentially became a study hall.

LESSONS LEARNED

The goals of these programs were to educate faculty and students about teen suicide, the warning signs, and steps to take to prevent a suicide. It was also an experiment in how to prevent suicides from occurring. Included in the presentation were two recurring messages that we emphasized throughout the process.

The first message: If you feel depressed and/or suicidal, help is available. We provided students with community resources and identified faculty and staff at each school, including the crisis teams, that students could seek out at any time.

The second message: Urge students to come forward if they have a friend or know of someone who is depressed and might feel suicidal. Recognizing that students might be reluctant to do this, we tried to clarify that this is not the same as "narcing" on someone who might have a stash of marijuana in their locker. This is potentially saving someone's life.

When discussing the second issue, two questions invariably came up. The first focused on concerns that if someone reported a friend and they were wrong, the friend might get angry with them. The second and more prevalent question centered around a situation where a friend might tell someone they were feeling suicidal but force them to promise not to disclose this information to anyone.

The answers to these questions were basically the same every time. If you inform someone about your concerns regarding a friend and it turns out to be wrong, the worst that could happen is that you might have someone get angry with you. The second scenario gets the same response. If you break someone's confidence, they might also get angry.

Here's the reality we chose to share directly to the students: "In either case, you may have a friend who's angry with you, but at least they're still alive."

We ran these programs for about five years. Staff turnover and other circumstances contributed to the program's end, but even so, we walked away knowing that we had created a heightened awareness of the issue in these schools.

Students who were at risk continued to be readily identified because of the faculty training we provided. The mechanisms we put in place to respond to those students became part of the institutional fabric of each campus.

As I mentioned, this all happened because three students committed suicide. During the time these programs were offered, we saw just one incident of a suicide attempt by a student. There may have been others, but we had no way of knowing, as they weren't documented.

Can we say definitively that the reduction in suicides and suicide attempts in this school district was directly related to these educational programs? Any researcher would tell you probably not. However, I think it is safe to say that these programs did have a positive effect, and while it may not have been the only factor in reducing suicides and suicide attempts, it certainly contributed to this positive outcome.

One more outcome needs to be mentioned. I said earlier that there were four high school campuses in this district, but we run the program in only three of them. The fourth campus contained the self-contained special education programs.

The district administration had initially determined that the program was not going to be presented to those students. I must admit that this was truly an oversight on our part. This decision was reversed, but only after the students in those programs insisted that they be included. These students were, in fact, among the most responsive. Another lesson learned.

THE DEBATE CONTINUES

Suicide prevention and education in schools have come a long way since then, but the debate continues regarding the responsibility of schools. I believe that suicide education should be mandatory in all schools. Whether that involves educating faculty and staff or providing programs for students and parents is a decision that should be made at the local level, but I firmly believe that ignoring the issue does only harm.

Our children are in school for about six hours a day, five days a week. Many of the warning signs for child and adolescent suicide are evident and can be identified by faculty and staff if they are properly trained.

Warning signs are not that hard to miss. For example, a drop in grades, acting out "bad" behaviors, chronic attendance problems, a lack of participation in class and related activities, or dramatic changes in behavior at school can all be signs of trouble. These are potential warning signs of a child or adolescent at risk, and school personnel need to be aware of these signs.

Recognizing warning signs is one part. School personnel also need to know what steps to take to help a student whom they believe is at risk.

It would be great if we could say that taking these steps and having procedures in place to address this issue would prevent a young person from committing suicide. Sadly, this is not the case. That said, I am not blaming schools for not doing enough to prevent suicide; they do not carry the sole responsibility for the safety of their students.

Responsibility for a death by suicide lies first and foremost with the individual. However, the responsibility for preventing suicide is shared among the individual, their family, peer group, school, community, including faith-based, workplace, the social service, and mental health systems, and social media.

Even law enforcement and the legal system have a certain responsibility when it comes to preventing suicide. All these entities play a role, and it is crucial that they all understand what they can do to prevent suicide.

19. SOME CLOSING THOUGHTS

BEFORE WE CLOSE, there are five important things to discuss.

1. THERE IS A DIFFERENCE BETWEEN SUICIDAL THOUGHTS/ FEELINGS AND A DEATH WISH.

A death wish goes something like this: "Sometimes, I wish a truck would run me over and kill me."

Suicidal ideation goes this way: "Sometimes, I feel like stepping in front of a truck."

A death wish may emanate from the same place as a suicidal ideation. The biggest difference is that it is more of a passive state, where one hopes for a catastrophe to happen instead of taking active steps to cause their own death. In the former situation, your assessment will be different than that of someone who is actively suicidal, but your intervention may be similar.

You'll still be dealing with feelings of hopelessness, helplessness, and worthlessness and trying to get at what brought the person to the point where they wish to die. Beyond that, as we discussed, your level of intervention, e.g., outpatient versus inpatient, etc., will be based on your determination of your client's level of risk, available resources, such as family and friends, and your ability to provide safety planning for the client as they progress through their treatment.

2. WHEN IT COMES TO SUICIDE RISK, THE MORE DANGEROUS TIME FOR A SEVERELY DEPRESSED CLIENT IS AS THEY ARE GETTING BETTER.

A severely depressed person cannot usually make even small decisions, much less create and carry out a suicidal plan for themselves.

As a client's depression begins to lift, through whatever means, their risk for suicide goes up. The client may feel better, but they are still depressed. As their depression lifts, they may then have the energy to carry out their suicide plan.

Therefore, throughout the course of treatment, it is important to continue to assess the client for suicide risk. As they improve even more, the risk for suicide diminishes, but, until then, that client is very much at risk.

I know of one tragic case. An eighteen-year-old young man, living with his parents, had been depressed for some time. He had made at least one suicide attempt and, as a result, was subsequently hospitalized in a private psychiatric facility.

After discharge, he was actively engaged in therapy with an outpatient therapist. A few months later, he showed encouraging signs of improvement. His mood was lifting, and he started to show a renewed interest in sports, which had always been his passion, and he was also doing much better in school.

His parents were still cautious, but one Friday evening, he convinced them he was fine and that they deserved a night out. He said he would just watch a game on TV and go to bed.

Feeling encouraged, his parents went to dinner and a movie. When they returned home, they found their son in the basement, dead from a self-inflicted gunshot to the head. They were devastated, but despite their feelings of guilt, sadness, and anger, they did eventually move on.

They spoke out about their experience to anyone who would listen. They also set up a foundation in their son's name to pay for suicide education and prevention programs in their community. Out of tragedy came hope.

3. ANOTHER RARE PHENOMENON, ACCORDING TO MY CRISIS INTERVENTION TRAINER IN COLLEGE, IS CALLED THE 'LIGHT BULB EFFECT."

This occurs in situations when an individual concludes that by committing suicide, they have found the answer to their problems. In a day, week, or whatever time schedule they have chosen, all their cares and worries will be gone, so why not feel better during the time they have left?

Such a scenario should be taken with more than a grain of salt. We need to be suspicious of clients who, for no apparent reason, suddenly appear to be feeling better. While we all want to applaud our clients for making progress, you need to explore why and how this is happening.

I have had clients say, "Thank you, but I will no longer be needing your services." They say they have figured out everything and have found the answer to their problems.

If this happens to you, be careful; that "answer" may be suicide. You need to ask why they suddenly feel so much better. The reason may not be because they just won the lottery.

4. IF YOU WORK IN THIS FIELD LONG ENOUGH, ODDS ARE, ONE OF YOUR CLIENTS WILL DIE BY SUICIDE.

If you work in mental health, you deal with at-risk people. I hope the above prediction never comes true for you, but if it does, there are steps you should take.

Find your own source of support. It could be family, friends, or colleagues. Just don't suffer alone in silence. We are good at taking care of others, but we are often lousy at doing the same for ourselves.

Seek out support from your agency supervisor or, if you are not a part of an organization, get support from someone in a similar position. Most organizations have protocols in place to address such an occurrence, and you may find yourself a part of an internal review.

That doesn't mean you did anything wrong. It simply means your organization is doing what it needs to do from a clinical perspective and checking for any potential liability.

Even after death, client confidentiality may still hold. Most states have regulations regarding this issue, and you should become familiar with them.

I recommend you do not talk to the media. A suicide can become big news, especially in small communities. You may not be able to provide information, due to client confidentiality, and you may not be in any shape to make a statement. Most organizations have policies regarding contact with the media. You or your supervisor should be aware of these policies and act accordingly.

Whether you attend a wake, funeral, or memorial service is up to you. Each circumstance is unique, and what may or may not be acceptable is up to you and your supervisor.

Be careful what you say and do. Sending flowers or sympathy cards to the family or apologizing could be misinterpreted as an admission of liability. Admitting to colleagues or acquaintances that you feel you are somehow at fault could also be construed the same way.

It's sad, but this is the reality of the world we live in. Talk to your supervisor. In most cases, contacting the family may be fine, and they may need to do some grief work with you or a colleague. Reaching out may help facilitate that process.

5. SEVERAL RELATED ISSUES HAVE NOT BEEN COVERED HERE, MAINLY BECAUSE I DO NOT FEEL I HAVE ENOUGH EXPERTISE IN THESE AREAS.

We have not discussed the phenomenon of cutting, especially among adolescents. An entire collection of research and information on *indirect self-destructive behaviors* is available. These behaviors include substance abuse, risk-taking behaviors, and even smoking. I would recommend that you seek out as much information as you can gather.

When it comes to the impact of trauma and PTSD, there is substantial research being conducted on the connection between head trauma and suicide, which I recommend you study.

With all these issues in mind, keep learning!

It's taken me almost fifty years to reach the point where I keep hearing or reading the same information over and over, just in slightly different formats. The more you read and the more workshops and seminars you attend, the closer you will get to that point.

Even now, I never fully believe I have learned it all. There's always something new out there. It just takes a little more digging than it used to. There is no such thing as a know-it-all. I am only a know-some-of-it.

I hope that I have expanded your knowledge of this complex and difficult subject. There will always be aspects that remain uncovered, which is exactly why you need to continue to learn.

Thank you.

About the Author

Tom Butero is a retired clinical social worker. He currently works as a consultant at the University of Massachusetts Medical School, where he assists in the development of training programs and exams leading to certification for the Child and Adolescent Needs and Strengths (CANS) tool by child mental health providers. He also provides consulting services to individual providers regarding CANS certification exams and participates in ongoing evaluations and updates of CANS training modules.

Tom received a master of social work degree and a bachelor of science degree in applied behavioral science, both from George Williams College in Downers Grove, Illinois.

Teaching assignments have taken him to Boston University School of Social Work, the University of Illinois School of Social Work, and Aurora University.

Suicide and suicide prevention has been his specialty for nearly fifty years. He has presented hundreds of workshops, seminars, and presentations on the subject and has also written several professional articles for various publications, including for the National Association of Social Workers.

References

Blos, Peter; (1966 1962. 269 s. 269 s.); *On Adolescence: A Psychoanalytic Interpretation*; The Free Press, New York.

Caplan, G. (1961); *An Approach to Community Mental Health;* Grune and Stratton, New York.

Caplan, G. (1964); *Principles of Preventive Psychiatry;* Basic Books, New York.

Drake, Robert et al.; "Suicide Among Schizophrenics: A Review"; *Comprehensive Psychiatry*, Volume 26, Issue 1, 90 – 100.

Durkheim, Émile; (1951); *Suicide: A Study in Sociology.* Translated by John A. Spaulding and George Simpson; The Free Press of Glencoe, Glencoe, Illinois.

Farberow, N. L. ;(1980). *The Many Faces of Suicide: Indirect Self-destructive Behavior*; McGraw-Hill, New York.

Farberow, Michael L. & Norman, L. & Litman, Robert E., editors; 1985; *Youth Suicide;* Springer Publications.

Farberow, N. L., & Shneidman, E. S.; (1965); *The Cry for Help* (1st McGraw-Hill pbk. ed.); McGraw-Hill, New York.

Fialko L, Freeman D, Bebbington PE, Kuipers E, Garety PA, Dunn G, Fowler D. Understanding suicidal ideation in psychosis: findings from the Psychological Prevention of Relapse in Psychosis (PRP) trial. Acta Psychiatr Scand. 2006 Sep;114(3):177-86. doi: 10.1111/j.1600-0447.2006.00849.x. PMID: 16889588.

Gurman, Alan and Kniskern, David, Ed.; *Handbook of Family Therapy. 2 vols.;* (1981 and 1991); (Ref RC488.5 H33); Brunner/Mazel, New York.

Kalisch BJ. Of half-gods and mortals: Aesculapian authority. Nursing Outlook. (1975) 23:22–8

Klagsbrun, F.; (1976); *Too Young to Die: Youth and Suicide*; Houghton Mifflin, Boston, MA.

Kroll, Jerome, MD: "No-Suicide Contracts as a Suicide Prevention Strategy,"; *Psychiatric Times*. Vol. 24 No. 8.

Kubler-Ross, E.; (1969); *On Death & Dying*; Simon & Schuster/Touchstone, New York.

Lindemann, E. ;(1944); *Symptomatology and Management of Acute Grief;* The American Journal of Psychiatry; 101, 141–148.

Lindemann, E.; (1979); *Beyond Grief: Studies in Crisis Intervention*; Aronson, New York.

Masterson, J. F. (1972); *Treatment of the Borderline Adolescent: A Developmental Approach;* John Wiley & Sons, New York.

Meeks, J. E. (1986); *The Fragile Alliance: An Orientation to the Psychiatric Treatment of the Adolescent* (3rd ed.); Krieger Pub. Co., Malabar, FL

Miller, N. S., Mahler, J. C., & Gold, M. S. (1991). Suicide Risk Associated with Drug and Alcohol Dependence. Journal of Addictive Diseases, 10(3), 49-61.

Mina M. Rizk & Sarah Herzog & Sanjana Dugad & Barbara Stanley, Suicide Risk and Addiction: The Impact of Alcohol and Opioid Use Disorders, Current Addiction Reports (2021) 8:194–207

Parad, H. J. (1965); *Crisis Intervention: Selected Readings*; Family Service Association of America, New York.

Selye Hans; "*The General Adaptation Syndrome and the Diseases of Adaptation*"; (1946); Journal of Clinical Endocrinology; 6 (no. 2) :119–131.

Suicide Prevention Resource Center (2011); "Understanding Risk and Protective Factors for Suicide: A Primer for Preventing Suicide."

White, Robert W. (1959); "Motivation Reconsidered: The Concept of Competence"; *Psychological Review*. 66 (5): 297–333

Yue Zhao, Richard Montoro, Karine Igartua, Brett D. Thombs (2009); "Suicidal ideation and attempt among adolescents reporting 'unsure' sexual identity or heterosexual identity plus same-sex attraction or behavior: forgotten groups." *Journal of the American Academy of Child and Adolescent Psychiatry* (Impact Factor: 6.97). 02/2010;49(2): 104-13. DOI: 10.1016/j.jaac.

www.ingramcontent.com/pod-product-compliance
Lightning Source LLC
LaVergne TN
LVHW041940070526
838199LV00051BA/2859